JECB 18:1 (2014): 1–136

Contents

Editors: David I. Smith and Trevor Cooling

Contributors

- **Diana Abbott** is associate professor of education at Roberts Wesleyan College (Rochester, New York).

- **Nathan F. Alleman** is assistant professor of higher education and student affairs at Baylor University (Baylor, Texas).

- **Patrick Allen** is a professor of higher education and leadership at George Fox University (Newberg, Oregon).

- **Ken Badley** serves as book review editor for the *Journal of Education and Christian Belief.*

- **Chris Cochran** serve as a school counselor at Options High School (Bellingham, Washington).

- **Matthew Etherington** teaches education at Trinity Western University (Langley, British Columbia).

- **Perry L. Glanzer** is professor of educational foundations at Baylor University (Baylor, Texas).

- **Elizabeth Groppe** is associate profesor of theology at Xavier University (Cincinnati, Ohio).

- **Dana Hanesova** is associate professor of religious education at the University of Matej Bel in Banská, (Bystrica, Slovakia).

- **Michelle C. Hughes** is assistant professor of education at Westmont College (Santa Barbara, California).

- **Aaron Imig** is assistant professor of education at Corban University (Salem, Oregon).

- **Nancy Johnson** teaches education at Geneva College (Beaver Falls, Pennsylvania).

- **William K. Kay** is professor of Pentecostal studies at the University of Chester (Chester, UK).

- **Randall King** teaches first grade at Gilbert Park Elementary School (Portland, Oregon).

- **Lisa Laurier** teaches education at Whitworth University (Spokane, Washington).

- **HeeKap Lee** teaches education in the Teacher Education Department, Azusa Pacific University (Azusa, California).

- **Anne Lumb** is a PhD student and associate tutor at the University of Nottingham (Nottingham, UK) and a diocesan schools adviser for the Diocese of Southwell and Nottingham.

- **Andrew Marfleet** is a retired school inspector and former chair of the Association of Christian Teachers in England.

- **Laurie Matthias** is associate professor and coordinator of graduate programs in education at Trinity International University (Deerfield, Illinois).

- **Karen Maxwell** is associate professor of education at Abilene Christian University (Abilene, Texas).

- **Eileen Mejia** teaches courses for the College of Arts and Sciences, the School of Business, and the School of Graduate Studies at Marylhurst University (Marylhurst, Oregon).

- **Andrew Morris** serves as research director at the Maryvale Ecclesiastical Institute (Birmingham, UK).

- **Sally Nash** is director of the Midlands Institute for Children, Youth and Mission at St John's College (Nottingham, UK).

- **Joe Olson** teaches education at Kentucky Christian University (Greyson, Kentucky)

- **Andrew Palfreyman** teaches mathematics at Twyford C. E. High School (Acton, UK).

- **Margie Patrick** is assistant professor of education at the King's University College (Edmonton, Alberta).

- **Pablo J. Santana** teaches educational administration and leadership at La Laguna University (Tenerife, Canary Islands).

- **Gordon T. Smith** serves as president and professor of systematic and spiritual theology at Ambrose University College (Calgary, Alberta).

- **Ros Stuart-Buttle** is senior lecturer in theology and education at Liverpool Hope University (Liverpool, UK).

JECB 18:1 (2014): 5–6   1366-5456

David I. Smith and Trevor Cooling

Editorial

This issue of the *Journal of Education and Christian Belief* opens with a piece that we would rather have continued to postpone: a tribute to Harro Van Brummelen, who recently passed away after an extended battle with cancer. The tribute, by Ken Badley and John Shortt, justly highlights Harro's great contribution to Christian education, which will continue in many an educational setting through his writings even as he enjoys in full the grace out of which he wrote.

In "Creating Confessional Colleges and Universities That Confess," Nathan Alleman and Perry Glanzer review the recent turn to a focus on practices in discussions of how faith informs pedagogy in Christian higher education and question the implications of this approach for practices at the institutional level. If Christian practices are to "infuse the life of the community" then they need to frame the work of administrators and the actions of institutions. Alleman and Glanzer focus in particular on the practice of confession, opening an exploration of what it might mean for institutions to adopt the practice. They distinguish different kinds of confessional practice, which they call "ritual" and "situational," and discuss examples of situations in which each kind of institutional response may be appropriate.

Elizabeth Groppe's contribution, "A Harvest of Humility," addresses ways in which the virtue of humility might be cultivated in Christian higher education in the context of agricultural experiences. While resisting an easy romanticizing of agricultural practice, Groppe suggests that combining sustained experience of agriculture with theological study can help cultivate humility in terms of a proper relationship to God and to creation.

Ann Lumb's article focuses on school support of children's spiritual development in the context of school inspection regimes in the United

Kingdom. Based on a year-long study of a Church of England Primary School, the article studies how the tensions caused by multiple inspection requirements become evident in the learning environment, particularly in terms of the relationship between a highly performative culture and children's exploration of spirituality. Lumb suggests implications for the kinds of support needed on the part of church school leaders.

Ros Stuart-Buttle turns our attention to the online learning context, focusing in particular on how the turn to online learning is to be interpreted theologically. Drawing from the practice of a continuing professional development program for adults taught online in the UK for the church school sector, Stuart-Buttle examines the interruptive dimension of online pedagogy as framed by Lieven Boeve's theology of interruption. Online pedagogy, it is argued, opens up new possibilities for "belonging, communicating, relating, being present, and sharing faith with others."

The papers in this issue range from the humility of agricultural labor in the fields to attempts to create learning communities in online environments, and from young learners exploring spirituality in a primary school to questions of how university administrators should relate to the practice of confession. Together they illustrate some of the breadth of contexts in which questions about the intersection of education and Christian belief are being pursued.

JECB 18:1 (2014): 7–8   1366-5456

News and Notes

ECCEN Conference: "Christian Education in Europe to 2020"

The European Conference for Christian Education in the Netherlands will host an English-language conference on September 24–26, 2014, for European school leaders, policy makers, consultants, politicians, and others who play a leadership role in education. *JECB* is proud to note that one of its previous editors, John Shortt, is scheduled to be among the featured presenters.

For more information, see www.driestar-educatief.nl/international -programmes/eccen-2014 for more information.

Contents of the Most Recent Issue of the *Journal of Christian Education*

Vol. 54, no. 2 (September 2011) has the following articles:

- Neil Holm, "Educating the Net Generation for Transnformation and Transcendence."
- John Mitchell O'Toole, "Religion, Politics, Science and Bureaucracy: An Australian Science Curriculum?"
- Siew Yap, "Teaching Bioethics: A Christian Approach in a Pluralistic Age"
- William Anderson, "Sin and Education"
- Reviews: Alister E. McGrath, *Surprised by Meaning: Science, Faith, and How We Make Sense of Things*; Les Ball,

Transforming Theology. Student Experience and Transformative Learning in Undergraduate Theological Education

Further information about *JCE* can be obtained from The Editor, *Journal of Christian Education*, PO Box 602, Epping, NSW 1710, Australia (e-mail: editorjce@acfe.org.au; URL: http://www.jce.org.au/index.php)

JECB 18:1 (2014): 9–11   1366-5456

Ken Badley (with John Shortt)
A Tribute to Harro Van Brummelen

January 7, 1942–January 15, 2014

In the fall of 1981, I agreed to teach a short course on education at Regent College in Vancouver the following January. Harro Van Brummelen's name appeared on the list of recommended guests that the previous instructor of the course had passed along to me. At that time, Harro was serving as director of the British Columbia Society for Christian Schools (CSI), and we arranged by telephone that he would speak to the class about Christian day school education.

When, some months later, Harro appeared on the Regent campus to speak, we realized that we were both enrolled in the same January-semester doctoral course at the University of British Columbia. As it turned out, all five students were connected in some way to Christian education, and the rather secular professor did not know what he had got into. Thus began a three-decade-long friendship and collegial relationship. Like many of Harro's friends and colleagues, I suspect I got more than I gave, and to this day I thank God for the gift that Harro was to me, to education, to the church, and to the world.

For several years in the 1990s, Harro served on the Education Commission of the Evangelical Fellowship of Canada, a group whose mandate was to support parents and educators in all kinds of schools. Harro carried deep in his DNA a commitment to Christian day schools, but he also believed deeply that parents and teachers connected to state schools needed support, and he unflinchingly gave his energy to help such parents and teachers work for the good of all children. Harro's own convictions found their roots deep in the Christian Reformed educational tradition, implying that he naturally affiliated with schools connected to Christian

Schools International (CSI). In fact, Harro studied these schools' history for his doctoral dissertation. But Harro willingly served all Christian schools, including those connected to the Association of Christian Schools International (ACSI), transcending what some have, at times, viewed as a boundary well worth defending.

His service to Christian educators reached well beyond North America. Ray Le Clair, regional director of ACSI's Former Soviet Union and Baltic States Region, reports that Harro was one of the biggest influences on his thinking about Christian education over the last couple decades. Harro advised Ray (and ACSI) on the aims, approaches, and mechanics of setting up a residential summer program for Christian teachers from all over the former Soviet sphere. Both in the 1990s and since the new millennium, Harro taught several courses for teachers in Russia and Ukraine, and has spoken at several conferences. *Walking with God in the Classroom* was translated into Russian in those early days of ACSI work in this region. *Walking* is now in its second Russian edition and, I'm told, remains the main book used by Christian educators there for an overview of Christian education. Recently a director of a Christian school showed Ray her very dog-eared copy of the book and said that she still uses it all the time. On a light note, Harro used long sentences, rendering translation somewhat of a challenge. By 2005 or 2006 Harro had mastered the translatable— shorter—sentence, making life easier for his translators. Harro also served in Western Europe and the UK, presenting keynote speeches at an early EurECA conference, at a Christian Schools Trust conference in the UK, and at ACSI events in central Europe.

For many years Harro led the teacher education program at Trinity Western University (TWU) in Langley, British Columbia, near Vancouver. These years were not without drama. From the first years of its program, Trinity Western's education graduates were required to follow their TWU program with a year's study in a public university so that they might be prepared properly for service in public classrooms, a policy that Trinity Western appealed in the courts. Because the case bore so directly on the rights of religious believers, as laid out in the Canadian Charter of Rights and Freedoms, the TWU case eventually made its way to the Supreme Court of Canada. That court decided that faith-based universities were in fact capable of preparing teachers who would function well in a diverse society. Harro led the education program through these challenging years, illustrating that he could stand by his firm convictions. But he also had a winsome manner; the British Columbia association of deans of education selected him as their chair for some years.

Most readers of this journal know Harro's books. Many have assigned one or another of this titles as a course text or in professional reading groups. When I reviewed the second edition of *Walking with God in the Classroom* for this journal, Harro told me that he had revised it mainly because so many state-school teachers had found it helpful (including those in Eastern Europe). Not having directed it toward state-school teachers originally, he was both surprised and pleased that it had found this audience, and so, to serve them better, he revised it. In an education course I teach annually at Tyndale University College in Toronto, I have used *Steppingstones to Curriculum* for some years. Year by year, students tell me that it is the clearest and most practical of the books I require them to read in the course. Clear, practical. These were Harro's concerns when we edited *Metaphors We Teach By* a few years ago. He had no interest in making his résumé longer; he wanted to equip teachers, as he often put it, "to think and teach like Christians."

Harro loved to create venues for conversation. In 1993 I proposed that the Institute for Christian Studies and Ontario Bible College (both of Toronto), Canadian Theological Seminary (then in Regina, Saskatchewan) and Trinity Western University sponsor "With Heart and Mind," a conference on Christian higher education in Canada, Harro suggested not one, but four, conferences. Such was the vision that gave energy to this person whom John Shortt has referred to as a "giant in the world of Christian education."

Thousands of educators have knowingly allowed Harro to shape their thinking. By implication, Harro has shaped hundreds of thousands of students, albeit without their knowledge. Harro worked hard, thought clearly, wrote prolifically, and gave much. We all remain in his debt. All who knew Harro will miss his smile and his wisdom. Those closest to him include his wife, Wilma; three children; ten grandchildren; and two sisters.

The Association of Christian Teachers welcomes enquiries from all Christians in education who are seeking fellowship with like-minded professionals.

All Christians in education are invited to sign up for our free email bulletin, ACTuality, which highlights education news, government policy initiatives, research findings, job related issues and purposeful spiritual resources as well as vacancies and events. There is also a prayer diary designed to stimulate and encourage the reader and pray-er. Simply send an email to subscribe@actforhim.org.uk together with your first and last names.

ACT is not a trade union nor a specialist counselling agency. However, members can obtain advice and support in their professional lives from experienced education practitioners by email and telephone.

ACT has a fully flexible roadshow called Every Teacher Matters and welcomes enquiries and invitations from local organisations who would like the roadshow to visit their locality.

For more information about the Association of Christian Teachers , contact our national office:
23 Billing Road, Northampton, NN1 5AT UK
or by telephone +44 (0) 1604 632046.
or via christians-in-education.org.uk/pages/contact

JECB 18:1 (2014): 13–28   1366-5456

Nathan F. Alleman and Perry L. Glanzer

Creating Confessional Colleges and Universities That Confess

Drawing upon the recent scholarly call to incorporate Christian practices into teaching, we contend that such practices should also be incorporated into the administration of Christian institutions. In particular, we explore the rationale for integrating the practice of Christian confession into the life of a university to address institutional sin. We then describe two types of confessional practice, ritual and situational, that perhaps should be grafted into the life of Christian educational institutions.

Key words: confession, practice, sin, higher education, colleges and universities, Christian

Recently, the conversation about the integration of faith and learning, or what we prefer to call the creation and redemption of learning and learners, has expanded in important, and we would argue, helpful ways. Although most Christian colleges and universities always understood the "Christian" element of their institutions as requiring daily or weekly chapel, maintaining Christian moral standards, and providing abundant opportunities for Bible students and prayer, the past few decades have seen increasing sophistication regarding the reasons for Christian faculty members to integrate faith and learning and the "confessional" nature of both secular and Christian learning (Marsden, 1997; Wolterstorff, 1999). Although there have been significant discussions about the need to expand or reframe this discussion, Christian scholars continue to produce a voluminous literature about how Christianity can and should inform scholarship (Jacobsen & Jacobsen, 2004; Smith, 2009; Glanzer, 2008; Ream & Glanzer, 2007).

James K. A. Smith's *Desiring the Kingdom* (2009) provides one of the recent noteworthy additions to this literature. Smith contends that we need "to re-envision Christian education as a formative rather than just an informative project" (p. 18). How we form and order our loves, he contends, should be the most important focus of life and of Christian education. We learn how to order our loves, Smith argues, through various worship practices or liturgies. These liturgies can be either religious or secular. For instance, shopping at a mall can be a secular liturgy that reinforces a certain kind of consumerism. To help counter deforming secular liturgies, Smith suggests that Christian practices embedded in a particular vision of Christian worship can shape our love and lives for the kingdom. For example, the liturgical calendar gives us an alternative sense of time; reciting God's law and announcing God's will for our lives "signals that the good is not something that we determine or choose for ourselves" (p. 170); and the practice of confession and assurance of pardon produces liberation.

In his closing chapter Smith (2009) contends that we also need to extend the application of these practices to wider university life. For instance, Smith suggests that in a residential college they could "include commitments to common meals; Sabbath observance; works of mercy in the neighborhood; weekly acts of hospitality for students, faculty, or those outside the university community; fasting together once a week; worship together at a local parish; a yearly service project; and more" (p. 226). We believe there is much to recommend from the approach offered by Smith. What we want to suggest in this essay is that Christian universities should also think about how to incorporate Christian practices not only into residential life but also into the classroom and the overall structure of the university, so that the practices of the church infuse the life of the community.

In this essay we will focus on the particular Christian practice of confession. Although universities may actually support a particular positive theological confession, in this article we will primarily refer to the form of confession that deals with the fallen aspects of life: the confession of sin. If we live our lives in light of the reality of the Christian story, we must recognize the fallenness of every academic discipline, institution, and practice. Although such recognition often takes place through the confession found in scholarship (e.g., Noll's *The Scandal of the Evangelical Mind* [1994]), we think it also needs to take place within the classroom and the university.

Consequently, we must think about how we might embed the practice of confession within the life of the university, as well as how we might allow for situations when special moments of confession may need to take place.

The corrosive effects of sin damage not only individuals but institutions as well; the question for Christian administrators and institutions is then one of process: recognizing our damaged condition and the promise of redemption at the institutional level. How do we move organizationally toward embracing this promised hope and healing? In this article we adopt and adapt the concept of *institutional confession*, drawing on the diverse fields of international politics, critical pedagogy, and Old Testament hermeneutics for description and insight. In the context of developing higher education administrators and faculty, we advocate for their role in developing *confessional colleges*, or institutions that make a corporate commitment to practices through which the acts of violence, oppression, neglect, abuse, and other moral failures resulting directly or indirectly from institutional policies, practices, and norms are owned and acknowledged, so that healing, altered behaviors, policies, and practices might commence.

The Practice of Confession

Depending upon the Christian tradition, corporate confession is often part of worship practices. James Smith (2009) points to the confession in the Anglican *Book of Common Prayer*, which the congregation recites while kneeling:

> Most merciful God, we confess that we have sinned against you
> in thought, word, and deed,
> by what we have done,
> and by what we have left undone.
> We have not loved you with our whole heart;
> we have not loved our neighbors as ourselves.
> We are truly sorry and we humbly repent.
> For the sake of your Son Jesus Christ,
> have mercy on us and forgive us;
> that we may delight in your will,
> and walk in your ways,
> to the glory of your Name. Amen.

Smith claims that confession within the Christian narrative and its understanding of reality involves recognizing a number of important dynamics that may not always be present if confession takes place outside such contexts. First, Smith emphasizes the relational nature of this confession. At its core, "the confession recognizes a failure to love—or rather, a failure to love well, to love rightly, to love the right things in the right order" (p. 177). Confession, it is important to note, is not merely a therapeutic exercise, although certainly it provides those emotional benefits. It ultimately concerns setting right one's relationship with the One to whom one confesses. Second, the content of God's ideal for creation provides the backdrop against which our lives are judged. Consequently, confession must involve not merely individual sins, but the ways in which we corporately build our lives, interact with nature, and build a culture that falls short of God's original intentions and design for human flourishing. Third, confession anticipates and only becomes complete through the pardon that we can receive from God, which is accomplished through the redemptive work of Christ. Through Christ, we can be forgiven by God. Confession anticipates the good news.

The Practice of Confession in the Classroom

The contributors to an edited volume by David Smith and James Smith (2011) discuss how Christian pedagogy could influence the methods one uses in the classroom. Although none of the contributors illustrate how confession might be applied in the classroom, we can certainly see how such a practice could be inserted at appropriate moments. For example, in one of our history classes, students read an article provocatively titled "One for the Crows and One for the Crackers: The Strange Career of Public Higher Education in Houston, Texas," by historian Amilcar Shabazz (1996). Shabazz describes the founding of two neighboring institutions, the University of Houston, and Texas Southern University, from the 1920s to the 1960s. The complex and in some ways contradictory position of education generally is evident through the social context of racism and segregation of the time: on one hand, education represented an opportunity for social and economic advancement, particularly at a time when African-Americans had few options. In this sense, education for the African-American population represented a potential threat to the White establishment. On the other hand, education represented a mechanism of control through which the Black population could be kept in subservient professions and away from White students. The Texas legislature ultimately founded two institutions with the hope of maintaining the guise of separate but equal education access. However, even after forced integration of the University of Houston, the local African-American community was divided over the future status of the institution that would later be known as Texas Southern University. Maintaining a separate university provided jobs for African-American faculty members and administrators and provided an opportunity for them to influence the curricula and development of young African-American intellectuals. Merging the two institutions would provide African-American students with better resources and, at least ostensibly, equal educational opportunity, though that was seldom the case in other contexts.

Shabazz's article takes on new meaning in the context of a history of higher education course, as part of a master's degree in a higher education and student affairs administration program in which both authors teach. After a discussion of the article, the class concludes analysis by mulling over possible residual effects of the context of institutional founding. Applying Colossians chapter 1, we consider the potential implications of Christ's redemptive work for "principalities and powers"—among them the structures, policies, and practices of organizations—that are by implication susceptible to the corrosive effects of human sin. We also think about what a redemptive imagination that recognizes Christ's lordship over *all* creation might bring to educational structures born of segregation and oppression. For example, given this history of racial tension, how might administrators experience the legacy of segregation within the institution and the local community, even decades later? How might it change local community relationships and economic development opportunities? How might it impact the ability to recruit and retain students and employees from certain racial or ethnic groups? In the context of this discussion, it might be appropriate to begin a time of confession regarding one's own experience of racism or one's experience of institutional advantage through racism (or bitterness from such disadvantage).

This vignette, set in a pedagogical context, highlights how organizationally embedded sin can linger generations removed from the initial decision-making occasion that produced it. In the following section we consider further the substance and implications of institutional confession that seeks to expose and root out sin. What might it mean for Christian administrators and faculty members to try to incorporate the practice of confession, not only in the classroom setting, but also in the life of the university?

Exploring Institutional Confession

Institutional confession requires stakeholders to alter their perspectives from a primarily individual-level agency orientation to a collective sense of ownership and responsibility. This step is necessary if institutional participants are going to take seriously the failings of colleges and universities as entities with a moral presence and culpability. To assist in this transition we offer perspectives from three disparate but interwoven areas, each with important contributions to this conversation: international politics (represented by Mark Amstutz), critical pedagogy (represented by Barry Kanpol), and Old Testament hermeneutics with a focus on the prophets (represented by Walter Brueggemann). We will then turn more specifically to the context of higher education and discuss implications for practice.

Correcting the Story: Institutional Confession in International Politics

In *The Healing of the Nations: The Promise and Limits of Political Forgiveness*, Mark Amstutz (2005) builds a case for what he terms "collective forgiveness," or corporate responsibility-taking in response to failings resulting from criminal, political, moral, or metaphysical (that is, indifference, neglect, or the failure to oppose evil) wrongdoing at the national level. Drawing on case studies set in Chile, Argentina, South Africa, and Northern Ireland, Amstutz asserts that although attempts at national-level confession and reconciliation have occurred with varying degrees of commitment and success, these attempts, when pursued earnestly and thoughtfully, represent the best alternative for healing and restoration:

> I argue that collective forgiveness is both possible and desirable. It
> is possible because forgiveness, while rooted in personal morality,
> is nonetheless applicable to the moral life of communities. And it

is desirable because it provides a way—indeed the only way—to overcome past wrongdoing through truth telling, remorse, and the implicit promise to not repeat the offense. Forgiveness lifts the moral burdens of past moral wrong-doing by "purifying" individual and collective memory through the deliberate moral act of viewing the past truthfully but without resentment or vengeance. The truth of the past is acknowledged, but through the morally courageous act of repentance and forgiveness, individuals and groups approach history redemptively. (p. 73)

In this passage Amstutz not only establishes the necessity of institutional confession and forgiveness, but identifies necessary elements that relieve both perpetrators and victims of the temptation of violence and retribution. Cleansing collective memory by moving toward reconciliation does not free the offenders, individually or collectively, of legal responsibilities according to Amstutz. Yet in practice some nations have found that encouraging truth telling is so important that legal and even moral preconditions were removed: in South Africa's postapartheid Truth and Reconciliation Commission, establishing a public record of wrongs was so important that offenders who confessed fully were granted absolution from criminal culpability and were not required to show remorse. Amstutz seems to advance the importance of institutional confession upon the assumption that institutional wrongdoing is almost always accompanied by attempts of the powerful to shroud the truth in a combination of false legitimacy and denial. For restoration to take place, institutions must first correct the historical record, legitimizing the claims of victims and thereby creating the basis for healing. Nevertheless, Amstutz's case studies also illustrate that collective confession is incredibly difficult work, often resisted by both perpetrators and victims. As Barry Kanpol's efforts illustrate in the next section, the will for confession must be accompanied by adequate preparation for and perspective on this collective process.

Naming the Offense: Institutional Confession in Critical Pedagogy

Most of Amstutz's work occurs in the past tense as nations critically examine occasions of injustice and speak the truth of these events to themselves and to the world. By contrast, Barry Kanpol (1994; 1998) is focused on the future: preparing public educators to encounter a system of structured power through which dominant groups and individuals maintain cultural, economic, and political hegemony. Much like our opening example of administrators in training, Kanpol is earnest in his desire for neophyte teachers to enter instructional positions fully aware of the power relationships that create and perpetuate disadvantage, of which they, by virtue of their professional role, are automatically a part. And, like Amstutz, Kanpol views personal and collective confession as essential aspects of addressing systemic injustice. Kanpol's focus is on the processes that precede institutional confession: self-reflection, dialogue across communities, empathy, and (borrowing from bell hooks) what she refers to as "testimony." Interpreting hooks, Kanpol (1998) suggests that testimony "means that we should all bear witness and/or openly own up to what our functions are in the social order, among other things" (p. 67). This reckoning is first of all a personal accounting for ways in which each of us participate in oppressive social structures, and the actions we can take to rectify the situation (although this characterization may oversimplify our degree of entanglement with these systems). However, closely linked to this individual process is one of institutional confession through which actors (teachers in this case), as moral representatives of educational systems also witness against the structures of inequality and oppression, among them race, resource differentials, gender assumptions, and other embedded metanarratives that systemically advantage some over others.

Kanpol (1998) adroitly notes that very little of this sort of self- and collective analysis occurs among teachers and within teacher education programs where new teachers are, by their own accounts, simply focused on doing a good job: "A teacher must have a conscious social vision that is more inclusive than 'I want to help kids, be the best teacher, see the light in kids eyes' etc. etc., to be an 'effective' or 'excellent' teacher" (p. 72). Although he does not press this point, Kanpol hints at the rich irony that professional "excellence" can serve as a cover for conformity to institutional expectations in which moral nerve can become a liability and an affront to the protection of systems that cast critique as a distraction from "putting students first." The temptation of the good soldier, whether in apartheid South Africa or in urban Philadelphia schools, is also present in behaviors of new college administrators or faculty: pleasing supervisors or tenure committees and filtering behaviors through the language of strategic plans and mission statements can quickly disallow critical perspective-taking under the guise of doing good, "student-centered" work.

Thus in Kanpol's (1998) assessment, institutional confession is rooted in a posture of skepticism and critical analysis taken by those who work in the system. This posture results "in a kind of reflective dialogue that is both gut wrenchingly honest and blatantly unpretentious" (p. 186). Both Kanpol and Amstutz emphasize the importance of truth-telling in their versions of institutional confession. For Amstutz institutional confession is "situational, occurring as occasions of abuse arise and requiring accompanying structures to process the identified transgressions. Kanpol suggests that confession is the spillover from an ontological commitment that joins unblinking self-assessment with unrelenting systemic critique. His version of confession positions it as part of an ongoing process of self-reflection and collective analysis. These two approaches to confession, and the orientations toward reconciliation that motivate them, have at least some of their roots in the tradition of the Old Testament prophets for whom care for nation and self was expressed through both ongoing and occasional reevaluation of the systems in which one participates.

Confession Opposed: Walter Brueggemann and the Old Testament Prophets

Institutional confession may, at this point, begin to seem attractive, refreshing, and liberating. However, laborers in higher education must keep in mind that the kind of deeply wrought collective soul-searching and truth telling urged by Amstutz and Kanpol may be seen as an affront to the preferred narrative and institutional identity projection so carefully crafted by our departments of admissions, development, athletics, public relations, university counsel, and others. Indeed, "the powers" (of which, Kanpol reminds us, educators are always members) often are uninterested in hearing the critique of the prophets and of truth tellers. In fact, as Old Testament scholar Walter Brueggemann argues, it is part of the established order's basic function to maintain a narrative of triumph, success, and stability that rejects and denies the grief that should accompany sin and its associated organizational corrosion. Brueggemann (1978) calls this ruling story the "royal consciousness," a pathos that is "committed to achievable satiation . . . it has created a subjective consciousness concerned only with self-satisfaction. It has denied the legitimacy of tradition that requires us to remember, calls us to care" (p. 42).

Applied to higher education, these strong words may seem like hyperbole. But participation in the institutional rankings game means playing by the rules set by a secular academia often unashamed to engage in the tripartite elements Brueggemann (1978) condemns as the *economics of affluence*, the *politics of oppression*, and the *religion of immanence and accessibility*. Kanpol reminds us of the temptation of doing good work that becomes a twisted justification for inattention to larger systemic corruption. Similarly, the pursuit of excellence—defined by metrics such as how many students an institution refuses to admit or how large an institution's endowment has grown—easily becomes a beauty pageant where national rankings set campus priorities and steer institutional image-making. In this environment, ethics are determined by legal counsel rather than a collective commitment to exposing the corrosive effects of our human failing to the light of Christ's forgiveness and reconciliation. At our own beloved institution, a recent standout year of athletic success led to loud proclamations of excellence that overshadowed a celebrated athletic program's recruiting violations. Such situations should cause administrative leaders and faculty to ask whether we are too quick to dismiss these violations as the results of poor individual choices rather than the products of the unseen systemic "royal consciousness" where, as Brueggemann (1978) puts it, "much *dancing* happens and where no *groaning* is permitted" (p. 42, emphasis in original). It is not then that our administrators (and faculty) are schemers undermining the virtues of us righteous ones. We are all imbued with this royal consciousness and deeply challenged to imagine another way of seeing, let alone another way of living. To expect anything different requires that we develop practices that reinforce an identity based on personal and institutional confession not as a grudging and hateful task set upon us, but as an essential element to being about something very different—the kingdom of God in the world.

Institutional Practice: Ritual and Situational Confession

With the imperative for confession in higher education established, we suggest that operationalizing this commitment requires two types of practice also reinforced by Amstutz, Kanpol, and Brueggemann: structures and processes that remind organizations of the need for regular confession, and organizationally self-imposed expectations that confession occur as important events require it. In the Catholic tradition the sacrament of confession includes an annual event of confessing with a priest (commonly around Easter), with the additional expectation that major moral infractions be confessed as they occur or are recognized. This template provides a useful framework for institutional confession as well, combining what we will call *ritual confession* (regular structured events) and episodic analysis (or what we refer to here as *situational confession*) that occurs as significant events, current and historical, are brought to light.

Ritual Confession

It will not take students long on any college campus to realize that the institution's marketing material failed to capture the whole reality at the institution. Not every professor cares deeply about students, not all students care deeply about others, and not every dimension of the institution reflects the highest standards of Christian excellence. Such an experience can easily lead students to cynicism, and certainly some faculty at Christian institutions who bear the wounds of these battles may be quite willing to guide them in that direction.

Such realities should not lead us to avoid favorable marketing or image-projection. We suppose that like the courtship process, one cannot and should not expect the hopeful suitor to start by revealing his or her imperfections. When pursuing or being pursued, we always put on the best face. Admissions efforts in the age of student consumerism are no different.

Nonetheless, a community that seeks to live out the Christian story must recognize that it will continually fall short of God's ideals. Although ritualized institutional confession provides no panacea, it does provide a space for all members of the community to reflect upon and voice the obvious recognition that every person and every cultural expression of our

23

academic community will fall short of God's ideals. Given the obviousness of individual as well as institutional shortcomings, the tempting move might be to accept the general truth of moral failing associated with our fallen human condition without taking the pains to identify and articulate specific points of transgression that are easier to ignore than to vet. However, the trio of Amstutz, Kanpol, and Brueggemann remind us that it is in truth telling that the temptation to gloss over corrupted behaviors is rejected. It is in truth telling that not only behaviors but systems of oppression are named and called into account. And it is in truth telling that the campus community strives to be a people for whom corporate confession is an important part of establishing and maintaining a distinctive identity.

On this final point, the practice of ritual confession offers several other benefits as well. First, it habituates faculty, administrators, and students to one of the fundamental practices of Christian community. Since the practice of confession reflects a reality of life, that we live in a fallen and broken world, we would argue, it should inform all of university life as well. In this case, we believe, some universities perhaps need to add a practice that might help them embody this part of the Christian story in their own corporate lives.

Institutional confession is an unusual practice within higher education. The peculiarity of the practice may also be its potency: modeling confessional behavior for students, employees, and other colleges and universities can be a witness to the power of Christ's transforming love, grace, and reconciliation and a call to pursue it throughout life. Amstutz (2005) notes how this effect came as a result of Pope John Paul II's leadership in Catholics' collective confession for past behavior toward various oppressed subgroups:

> By acknowledging that Catholics had periodically strayed . . . the Pope was providing a model of collective healing. In effect, by publicly confessing the church's moral failings, the Pope was inviting individuals and collectives to undertake a comparable process of accountability, truth-telling, and repentance in the hope that such actions would "purify memory" and thereby create a new foundation for the moral restoration of persons and communities. (p. 74)

Embracing institutional confession not only models good practice to others, but also introduces the humility of institutional critique. Christian colleges and universities interested in pursuing ways of living out the ideals embedded in their particular narratives will also be the ones that say to their students, "We need your help, and you too can offer critique of this university that helps us come closer to living out our ideals." Too often, colleges and universities that are associated with a particular Christian tradition are also associated with being more authoritarian or centrally governed. By contrast, we think it is possible that such institutions are not necessarily Christian in their commitments or practices, but rather in a parochial culture they are seeking to perpetuate. By virtue of their commitment to a particular understanding of the Christian tradition, Christian colleges and universities are places where freedom abounds as a result of their efforts to practice Christian confession. Institutional members here know they are not perfect, but with God's grace they are able to more closely live out their identity as a people created in God's own image. Although we would like to end with some institutional examples of Christian colleges and universities that engage in this practice, we do not know of any. We hope we are merely ill-informed. While we are aware of institutions where the ritual practice of revival involves an emphasis upon individual confession, we do not know of an institution that engages in a ritual form of confession.

Situational Confession

Kanpol's perspective that collective confession be rooted in an orientation toward critique as an ongoing practice reinforces the importance of ritual confession. Amstutz's work focuses on actions taken by those in power or in the name of powerful organizations. His approach highlights situations that require the development of formal mechanisms to manage the confession process and group implications, as well as the arrival at an official posture that acknowledges wrongdoing as part of the conciliation process. Joining the two, Brueggemann's prophetic accusations represent an act of and call for situational confession brought about in part by the accumulated neglect of ritual confession.

Amstutz's review of national contexts adds needed detail to our understanding of the situations that call forth times of corporate confession.

Situational confession becomes an option (or perhaps a necessity) in three categories of circumstances analogous (in type, though seldom in degree) to ones that occur in higher education. In the first, collective confession came about when the oppressive, corrupt, or amoral leadership and control held by a person or group ended and a collective dialogue seeking restoration could occur. Many of Amstutz's examples, including the end of apartheid in South Africa, fit these criteria. Second, situational confession should occur when covert abuses are revealed and the nation or group seeks accountability and healing through means other than or in addition to legal retribution. A recent example at the university level occurred at Emory University, where 65% of the Jewish students at the dental school flunked out during the tenure of a particular dean between 1948 and 1961. When this was brought to light, Emory University invited the former students to the university and officially apologized. Emory Vice President Gary Hauk confessed, "Not to have acknowledged this shameful chapter in our history would be to live a lie" (Loftus, 2012).

Third, situational confession occurs when a nation or organization comes to understand past justified behavior as inappropriate and indefensible given current moral, ethical, or legal perspectives. In 2008 Bob Jones University apologized for its racist policies of the past. The university did not begin admitting black students until the 1970s and maintained an interracial dating ban until 2000. Their statement read, "For far too long, we allowed institutional policies regarding race to be shaped more directly by that ethos than by the principles and precepts of the Scriptures. We conformed to the culture rather than provide a clear Christian counterpoint to it. In so doing, we failed to accurately represent the Lord and to fulfill the commandment to love others as ourselves. For these failures we are profoundly sorry" (Parham, 2008).

Just as overt displays of racism have largely given way to more subtle and systemic forms, so the effects of institutional brokenness in need of confession may be encoded within institutional culture and climate rather than in official public policies and procedures. In student life, these values and behaviors may, for example, live on in the traditions of student organizations where unspoken norms discourage invitations of membership to those who are not White and wealthy, reducing the richness of a more diverse and challenging student experience. In academic administration they may be reflected in hiring processes that never quite seem to attract viable minority candidates because institutional leadership is reluctant to make changes that might upset important alumni or donors. Although many of these illustrations focus on structural racism, other examples of university life where the effects of institutional sin in need of confession could occur include labor practices (pay and working conditions for hourly employees and contingent employment faculty), athletics funding, endowment investments, and admissions and financial aid practices.

Of course, the difficult question when thinking about situational confession concerns the particular cases in which it is required. Students and disgruntled faculty or alumni will likely be only too happy to create a list of sins for which an institution should confess wrongdoing. Furthermore, some sins will perhaps hold greater cultural weight at a given moment, but other sins may go unacknowledged. The larger secular public may even hold up a Christian institution for a "sin" (e.g., failing to admit non-Christians or enforcing policies regarding the sexual behavior of students or employees) that perhaps represent principles that should be defended. Furthermore, even where there is clarity or agreement about sin, other restrictions may hinder the process. For example, FERPA (a federal privacy act protecting students) laws, negotiated settlements, or ongoing court proceedings may hinder what institutional leaders are able to say publicly about an occasion of harm. We freely acknowledge that discerning what incidents deserve this type of public confession will prove difficult. Factors of scope and magnitude (how widespread or egregious the behavior is) may offer some guide, but ultimately no formula for discernment can displace the importance of attentiveness to the Holy Spirit, the prophetic voices among us, and sensitivity to our own God-given conscience.

Conclusion

Like individual confession, institutional confession is essential to the health and flourishing of all parties involved on a grander level. This practice for Christian institutional life and flourishing, like proper individual life, is not simply a practice carried out for its own sake, but is embedded in a way of being in the world that rejects the lure of easy gains, selfish motives, and xenophobic reactions against the exploitable *other* among us. Being the kingdom of God in and through our brokenness will require our institutions and us to expect and be prepared to answer for our failing moments and to do so knowing that this confession is heard by a forgiving God.

References

Amstutz, M. R. (2005). The healing of nations: The promise and limits of political forgiveness. New York: Rowman & Littlefield.

Brueggemann, W. (1978). The prophetic imagination. Minneapolis: Fortress.

Glanzer, P. L. (2008). Why we should discard the integration of faith and learning: Rearticulating the mission of the Christian scholar. *Journal of Education and Christian Belief 12*(1), 41–51.

Jacobsen, D. G., and Jacobsen, R. H. (Eds.). (2004). Scholarship and Christian faith: Enlarging the conversation. New York: Oxford University Press.

Kanpol, B. (1998). Confession as strength: A necessary condition for critical pedagogy. *Educational Foundations, 12*(2), 63–75.

Kanpol, B. (1994). Critical pedagogy: An introduction. Westport, CT: Bergin & Garvey.

Loftus, M. (2012, October 15). Film screen acknowledges dental school bias. Emory News Center. Retrieved from http://news.emory.edu/stories/2012/10/er_dental_school_apology/campus.html.

Marsden, G. M. (1997). The outrageous idea of Christian scholarship. New York: Oxford University Press.

Noll, M. A. (1994). The scandal of the evangelical mind. Grand Rapids, MI: Eerdmans.

Parham, R. (2008). Bob Jones University apologizes for racist policies. Ethicsdaily.com. Retrieved from http://www.ethicsdaily.com/bob-jones-university-apologizes-for-racial-policies-cms-13489.

Ream, T. C. & Glanzer, P. L. (2007). Christian faith and scholarship: An exploration of contemporary developments. ASHE-ERIC Higher Education Report. Jossey-Bass: San Francisco.

Shabazz, A. (1996). One for the crows and one for the crackers: The strange career of higher education in Houston, Texas. *The Houston Review, 18*(2), 124-143.

Smith, D. I., & Smith, J. K. A. (Eds.). (2011). Teaching and Christian practices: Reshaping faith and learning. Grand Rapids, MI: Eerdmans.

Smith, J. K. A. (2009). Desiring the kingdom: Worship, worldview, and cultural formation. Grand Rapids, MI : Baker Academic.

Wolterstorff, N. (1999). Reason within the bounds of religion (rev. ed.). Grand Rapids, MI: Eerdmans.

JECB 18:1 (2014): 29–40   1366-5456

Elizabeth Groppe

A Harvest of Humility: Agrarian Practice and Christian Higher Education

Humility, the keystone of the virtues in the Christian spiritual tradition, has been dismissed by modern philosophers, critiqued by feminist theologians, and overpowered by our industrial and technological culture. The incorporation of agricultural experience in Christian higher education presents the opportunity to cultivate anew the virtue of humility, properly understood not as a practice of self-abnegation but as a relation of the creature to the God who has gifted us with nourishing soil and deified us in Christ.

Key words: virtue, humility, pride, agrarianism

"You can toss them in with a salad," Mary Lu said, reaching down and breaking off several tall, thin, emerald-green leaves of a garlic plant, "or sauté them with vegetables." Her hair was pulled into a neat bun and tucked underneath her cap. She wore sturdy boots, a long-sleeved cotton shirt, and khaki pants, and she carried a hoe. Mary Lu Lageman is the director of farm operations at Grailville in Loveland, Ohio, and on this June day she stood among the lush rows of garlic in Grailville's kitchen garden, explaining to a group of Xavier University faculty participants in an agriculture workshop that the scapes of garlic must be cut in order to allow the plant to concentrate its energy in the formation of a plump bulb.

Mary Lu came to Grailville in her youth when she joined the Grail, an international Catholic lay women's organization. At that time, Grailville was a Grail project in Ohio, a farm run entirely by women who integrated liturgical prayer, agricultural labor, study, and the practice of fine arts (Kalvin, 1999). Today, Grailville is a retreat center and host to a community-supported agriculture program. Like the rings of a tree that mark each year of its growth, the lines on Mary Lu's hands testify to her wealth of experience. She speaks with a calm ease about the work of gradually building up the organic content of the soil of this kitchen garden that provides nourishment for those who come to Grailville for spiritual renewal. There is an aura about her—she is strong, dignified, and humble.

The workshop that brought Xavier faculty to Grailville's kitchen garden is just one of the many signs of the burgeoning interest in agriculture within higher education today, and the gardens and farms that are mushrooming on or near college and university campuses all around the country present new opportunities for faculty, staff, and students in Christian institutions of higher education to cultivate humility.[1] As Mark Schwehn observes, this spiritual virtue is a precondition of learning (Schwehn, 1993). The practice of humility enables us to acknowledge that we do not know everything, that our assumptions may be mistaken or inadequate, and that the cultivation of wisdom is a life-long vocation. In this article I discuss the foundational role of humility in the Christian spiritual tradition, modern critiques of humility, theological responses to these critiques, and the potential of agrarian practices to contribute to the cultivation of humility by drawing us into an encounter with the signs of the mysteries of creation and redemption that are hidden in the darkness of the soil.

Humility as the Ground of Virtue

Humility is not enumerated among the cardinal and theological virtues, but it suffuses justice, prudence, temperance, fortitude, faith, hope, and charity like the soil in which these virtues grow. From the deserts of Egypt to the hills of Subiaco, masters of the Christian tradition have identified humility as a foundation of the spiritual life. Abbot Anthony, the son of peasant farmers who entered the solitude of the desert in 285 CE and is now known as the father of Christian monasticism, made his way through the desert with humility at his side. "Who can get me through such snares?" he cried out in the face of temptation's cunning. "Humility," a voice responded (Ward, 1975, p. 2). Abba Poeman, another desert father, compared humility to the air without which we cannot survive.

"As the breath which comes out of his nostrils," he said, "so does a man need humility and the fear of God" (Ward, 1975, p. 173).

One century after Anthony entered the desert, Augustine probed the fabric of Roman culture and the motivations of his own actions and found *superbia* (pride) at the root of human sinfulness and the warping of social relationships. *Superbia* is the insidious temptation to put our own selves in a place that belongs rightly only to God. This primal sin typically takes subtle forms, such as the practice of virtue twisted by self-satisfaction, or the ordering of our relationships by a self-serving hierarchy of utility that supplants the divinely intended order of creation, as evident, for example, in a society that values an inanimate object (e.g., money) over human life (Cavadini, 1999). Augustine found a healing balm for *superbia*'s wounds in the compassion of the Word of God who took flesh in Jesus Christ, sacrificing his life on the cross for sinful humanity. Beholding the love of one who, "though he was in the form of God, did not regard equality with God as something to be exploited" (Phil. 2:6 NRSV), Augustine was moved to conversion. Baptized into Christ's body, Augustine's desires were reordered, and he sought no longer to gain the accolades of imperial Roman society but to give praise to the one "from whom [we] receive whatever in [us] is rightly deserving of praise" (Augustine, trans. 1972, p. 213). Augustine, John Rist explains, recognized that the human being "is not God but that he depends on God for his existence. . . . At bottom, humility is honesty about the human condition, and it is on the basis of that honesty, that willingness to face the facts, that man's moral and spiritual regeneration has to be founded" (Rist, 1994, p. 190).

Humility is the subject of the longest chapter of the *Rule of Saint Benedict* (ca. 530–560), and, according to Benedictine Columba Stewart (1998), it is in many ways the very heart of this guide to the cenobite life that became so influential not only within Benedictine communities but in the Christian tradition more broadly. Benedict's exhortation to humility outlines the steps that lead like the rungs of Jacob's ladder from fear of God and self-recognition of sinfulness ("I am a worm") to the perfect love that casts out fear (Benedict, trans. 1981, pp. 191–203). Community life nurtures progress in this spiritual ascent, schooling monks and nuns in an accountability to others that leads to a deeper and deeper awareness of God, in whom the heart expands "with the inexpressible sweetness of love" (pp. 164–166).

31

The liturgical life of the monastery is foundational to this spiritual growth, as is the manual labor that the rule requires. Ultimately, Benedictine Michael Casey explains, one learns truth through the practice of the rule—not truth in a merely intellectual sense but truth as a quality of being. Monastic life unmasks the falsehoods of human pretensions and embodies the truth that we are not gods but sinful creatures. The discipline of monastic life and the gift of the Spirit can make the practice of virtue habitual, at which point it becomes *natura* and then ultimately *gratia*, delight in perfect love (Casey, 2001). In the dramatic *Ordo Virtutum* written by Benedictine Hildegard of Bingen (1098–1179) and enacted by the women of her Rhineland community, Lady Humility leads the virtues as their queen.

Humility Decried and Defended

The philosopher David Hume (1711–1776) denounced humility as one of the "monkish" virtues—a virtue that those of good sense will recognize to be, in truth, a vice that stupefies understanding, hardens the heart, and sours the temper. He placed humility in the same category as celibacy, fasting, penance, mortification, self-denial, silence, and solitude (Hume 1776). Friedrich Nietzche's *Genealogy of Morals* (1887) described humility as a virtue of the slave.

Humility, indeed, can be a problematic ideal for women and men who have been colonized or subjected to slavery. Persons taken in chains from Africa to the United States, M. Shawn Copeland reminds us, were exhorted to be humble to their masters, and enslaved women were expected to submit to the sexual advances of white male slaveholders as well as slave catchers, slave traders, and the slave masters' adolescent sons (Copeland, 2002, p. 190). In this context the Christian tradition's exhortation to humility can have radically different connotations from those originally intended by desert fathers or Benedictine monks.

Valerie Saiving's influential 1960 article, "The Human Situation: A Feminine View," argued that the Christian ideal of humility is problematic for women at large. The historic predominance of men in the discipline of Christian theology, she explained, shaped theologies of sin and grace in a manner that reflects the male developmental process. Boys undergo a separation from the mother in order to establish a male identity and typically experience anxiety about their passage into manhood, which they attempt to overcome through self-magnification. Consequently, the sins to which men are prone are sins of pride and will-to-power. For women, in contrast, whose maternal role requires perpetual self-giving, the primary temptations are distractability, diffuseness, dependence on others for self-definition, and "in short, underdevelopment or negation of the self" (Saiving, 1979, p. 37). Humility is the antidote to male self-magnification but not to the self-negation of the female.

Saiving's work has inspired a careful analysis of the meaning of humility in theological literature. In a study of Mechthild of Magdeburg's *The Flowing Light of the Godhead*, for example, Michelle Voss Roberts notes the layers of complexity in the thirteenth-century Beguine's account of the soul's journey to God, a journey in which humility drives Mechthild's soul to a veritable abyss, "the spot where she can go no further: under Lucifer's tail" (Voss Roberts, 2009, p. 51). Voss Roberts affirms with Carolyn Walker Bynum that medieval women appropriated some of the negative images of women common in their culture. Mechthild, for example, describes herself as a "lowly crow" and "foul cesspool." This language reflects the subordinate place women were expected to assume in medieval society. At the same time, Mechthild's consciousness of sin does reflect a truth about the fallible human condition, and her humility grounds her relationship to God in this realism. Moreover, the humility that carries her under Lucifer's tail also her gives her authority to speak and carries her into the divinizing love of the triune God through Christ who inclined "exceedingly low beneath his nobility" (Voss Roberts, 2009, p. 68). Humility, paradoxically, is the staircase both down into the abyss of our depravity and up into the embrace of God. For Christian women mystics, Grace Jantzen affirms, humility ultimately "has to do with accepting and receiving the overwhelming love and delight of God in us, not with being ashamed of who and what we are" (Jantzen, 1995, p. 158).

Contextualized reflection on the complex layers of the meaning of humility in theological literature is a constructive response to the perception that humility is a monkish virtue, a slave morality, or a virtue more appropriate for the spiritual journey of the male than the female. In and of itself, however, the development of nuanced theologies of humility does not change the reality that we are members of a secular industrial civilization whose assumptions about the power of human knowledge and technology deny the realities of our creaturehood. "It is extremely difficult to argue the case for humility in our time," observes Norman Wirzba, professor of ecology, theology, and rural life at Duke Divinity School (Wirzba, 2008, p. 226). Our globalized industrial civilization has degraded soils, poisoned rivers, extinguished species, and destabilized the climate in a veritable rebellion against this queen of the virtues. "The evidence is clear," Wirzba continues, "that our desire to control the world and to engage it on our terms has led to its ruination. We are in need of a better way, a way that is more faithful and true to the biblical mandate to serve and keep creation" (Wirzba, 2007, p. 263).

"You are dust," says the priest, placing ashes on the foreheads of penitents in the Roman Catholic Ash Wednesday liturgy, "and to dust you shall return." These words recall the first chapters of the book of Genesis, a narrative in which God created *adam*, the first human being, from arable land, *adamah* (Gen. 2:7). Each time a speaker of Hebrew hears the name *adam*, he or she is reminded by this very word that human beings are made of *adamah* (soil), a truth about our origins that is lost in English translation. The Latin language is instructive in other ways. *Humus* (earth) is the root of the word *humilis* (humble).

In an essay provocatively entitled the "The Dark Night of the Soil: An Agrarian Approach to Mystical Life," Wirzba invites us to enter intentionally and intimately into the mystery of the *humus* from whence we come. Setting aside computers, cell phones, and other amenities of our urban civilization to turn compost or dig potatoes, we may find ourselves astonished at the complexity of a reality that we do not and cannot fully understand. In just one teaspoon of healthy soil, there may be one billion bacteria, several yards of fungal filaments, and scores of nematodes and protozoa. We are, writes Wirzba, "far from being able to name completely (let alone comprehend) the world as the site of grace and hospitality and mystery" (Wirzba, 2007, p. 263). We are "daily implicated in the life and death-wielding ways of creation," drawing our breath from microorganisms, plants, and other animals, living "through the sacrifices and kindnesses of others" (Wirzba, 2008, p. 226).

Wirzba's account of a human race that has overstepped its limits is hauntingly similar to Augustine's account of the *superbia* of fourth-century Roman society. Fascinated and attracted by the projects and power of our industrial and technological society, we have reordered and reshaped creation in service of our selves. Augustine's heart was moved to conversion by the compassion of God whose Word became incarnate in Jesus Christ, and Wirzba is moved also by the Wisdom of God hidden subtly within the life of the soil that intimate the paschal character of the economy of redemption. "The resurrection of the wheat," wrote Walt Whitman of a buried seed, "appears with pale visage out of its graves" (Whitman, 1881, p. 286).

We have lived by the assumption, reflects Wendell Berry, that human domination will produce a culture good both for us and for the world. "And now, perhaps very close to too late, our great error has become clear. . . . We have been wrong. We must change our lives" (Berry, 1968, p. 20). Berry, a Kentucky farmer, poet, and essayist calls for the development of new forms of culture that cooperate with the processes of the world and learn to yield to its limits. Even more importantly, Berry emphasizes, "we must learn to acknowledge that the creation is full of mystery; we will never entirely understand it. We must abandon arrogance and stand in awe. We must recover the sense of the majesty of creation, and the ability to be worshipful in its presence. For I do not doubt that it is only on the condition of humility and reverence before the world that our species will be able to remain in it" (Berry, 1968, p. 20).

The humility of which Wirzba and Berry speak is not a slave morality but an awareness of the truth of our existence before God. It is the awareness that we are *creatures*—that, as Augustine said, citing the words of the psalmist, "We did not make ourselves" (Augustine, trans. 1991, p. 172). "Theirs," writes Annie Dillard, beholding the mountains Tinker and Brushy, McAfee's Knob and Dead Man during her pilgrimage to Virginia's Tinker Creek, "is the one simple mystery of creation from nothing, of matter itself, anything at all, the given" (Dillard, 1994, p. 282). Have we really fathomed what it means to be *created*? To have somehow been loved from utter nothingness into being?

Encounter with the utter mystery of creation leads to a humility expressed not in self-deprecation but in awe and exuberant praise. "Praise [the LORD], sun and moon; praise him, all you shining stars! Praise him, you highest heavens, and you waters about the heavens! Let them praise the name of the Lord, for he commanded and they were created" (Ps. 148:3–5 NRSV). The glory that we give to God is not a denial of created goodness. "There is here," Jennifer Herdt explains, "no zero-sum game, no competition in which if one is honored, another is denied honor. To see things in that way is to have a false sense of humanity as standing over against God, rather than as issuing from God's creative love and destined for participation in the divine life" (Herdt, 2009, p. 553).

Agriculture as a School of Humility in Christian Higher Education

A growing movement to integrate the study and practice of agriculture into higher education presents new opportunities to bring teachers and students into contact with the created goodness of the earth. Although agricultural degree programs remain concentrated in the public land grant institutions established by Congress in the Morrill Act of 1862, more than 100 institutions of higher education in North America now have campus gardens or farms, and courses on topics such as "Food, Agriculture, and Society" and "Farm to Fork" are oversubscribed. In *Fields of Learning: The Student Farm Movement in North America*, Laura Sayre and Sean Clark survey this development, sharing accounts of how and why schools as diverse as Kentucky's Berea College and Yale University developed campus farms and gardens. Programs on these sites are integrating the theoretical knowledge of the mind and the practical knowledge of the body, fostering contextual knowledge and place-based learning, and cross-fertilizing the disciplines of biology, anthropology, history, theology, economics, English, and engineering. College farms and gardens also provide fertile ground for the cultivation of the virtue of humility.

In reflecting on their experience with college and university farm programs, several contributors to the volume *Fields of Learning* make reference to humility. Tim Crews of Prescott College, for example, writes of his experience with Jenner Farm: "If farming is anything, it is humbling. No sooner does a student succeed at raising a beautiful crop of chilies than blister beetles move through it like General Sherman's army, leaving complete destruction in their wake" (Sayre & Clark, 2011, p. 219). Agricultural work makes us acutely aware that we are not masters of creation and heightens cognizance of the limitations of our theoretical reasoning. It has been Crews's experience that topics that can appear to be black-or-white issues in the classroom—such as debates about agrochemicals—are complexified by actual agricultural experience.

Josh Slotnick of Garden City Harvest Farm, a project of the University of Montana's Program in Ecological Agriculture and Society, speaks of humility in a different sense:

> When people work in small groups engaged in humble labor, work that gets you dirty and doesn't require highly specialized abilities—the social barriers that naturally separate us from one another quickly erode. When you are weeding carrots across from someone, you both become dirty and sweaty, and you soon realize that you can work carefully and still have mental energy for conversation. One bed of carrots, and you will know where your partner is from, why he or she is here, and what he or she hopes to do next. The humility of the task creates common ground, and once you are standing there together on common ground, a recognition of one another's humanity is inevitable. (Sayre & Clark, 2011, p. 237)

Those of us who stand on the privileged side of the divisions of class, ethnicity, and gender that fragment our society readily see ourselves as superior to other persons, and in so doing, Augustine enables us to see, we replace the order of divine love with a self-serving utilitarian scale of value. Men and women, students and faculty, African-Americans and Euro-Americans who sow seeds and cull weeds together have the opportunity to grow in consciousness of our common creaturehood before God.

Norman Wirzba works with students on the Duke campus farm, and it is his experience that caretaking of the earth contributes directly to the formation of virtues, most notably humility and gratitude. The very physical posture that working in a field requires signifies "a humble disposition that is prepared to learn from creation and is willing to be taught by it in the ways of interdependent living" (Wirzba, 2007, p. 263). Attuned to the drama of the soil, students and faculty learn that our lives are maintained by a beneficence and grace that we neither command nor control. We live by God's good gifts, and in gardens and farms we can learn this truth not just intellectually but somatically and corporeally. The virtues of humility and gratitude "often run the risk of becoming abstract and vague, pious ornaments to an otherwise arrogant or rapacious life, because they do not grow out of our lived experience. There is an important difference between a virtue that one claims for oneself through speech and a virtue that grows spontaneously with practical experience" (Wirzba, 2003b, pp. 31–32).

One should not romanticize agricultural labor, which does not automatically make saints of everyone who picks up a hoe. Surveying what remains of Mattfield Green, Kansas, a town that like so many other rural communities has lost population in the latest stage of what Wendell Berry calls the "unsettling" of America (Berry, 1997), Wes Jackson reflects: "I know that this town and the surrounding farms and ranches did not sponsor perfect people. I keep finding whiskey bottles in old outhouses and garages, stashed between inner and outer walls here and there. . . . I hear the familiar stories of infidelities fifty years back. . . . [T]he human drama goes on" (Jackson, 1996, p. 97). Agricultural work is no guarantee of virtue. It is, however, a near-guarantee of sore muscles, calloused hands, and the periodic tragedies of crops lost to hail, blight, drought, or other calamities. Farming has always been a physically difficult and precarious enterprise and will be increasingly so in our era of climate change. Short visits to farms cannot really engage these realities and may be nothing more than a privileged form of agricultural tourism. But classes and programs that complement sustained agricultural experience with theological reading and reflection can contribute to the cultivation of humility. Sowing squash, hoeing beans, and digging our hands into the moist black richness of healthy soil, we learn experientially the truth of our common creaturehood before God and witness tangible signs that point us toward the paschal mysteries of creation and redemption. The humility that I beheld in the person of Mary Lu Lageman was neither a slave morality nor a form of self-abnegation. Rather, it was a humility rooted in the hidden ground of God's love from which she drew great strength and virtue.

Notes

1. This is part of a renewed national interest in agrarianism. On contemporary agrarian thought, see, for example, Berry (1997); Bahnson and Wirzba (2012); Davis (2009); Freyfogle (2001); Wirzba (2003a). For a critique of a proposal to require the integration of work in gardens within school curricula, see Jayson Lusk (2013).

References

Augustine. (1991). *Confessions.* (Henry Chadwick, Trans.). New York: Oxford.

Augustine. (1972). *The city of God.* (Henry Bettenson, Trans.). Middlesex, UK: Pelican.

Bahnson, F., and Wirzba, N. (2012). *Making peace with the land: God's call to reconcile with creation.* Downers Grove, IL: Intervarsity Press.

Benedict. (1981). *The rule of Saint Benedict.* (Timothy Fry, Ed.). Collegeville, MN: Liturgical Press.

Berry, W. (1968). A native hill. *The Hudson Review, 21,* 601–634.

Berry, W. (1997). *The unsettling of America: Culture and agriculture.* San Francisco: Sierra Club.

Casey, M. (2001). *A guide to living in the truth: Saint Benedict's teaching on humility* . Liguori, MO: Liguori.

Cavadini, J. C. (1999). Pride. In A. Fitzgerald and J. C. Cavadini (Eds.), *Augustine through the ages: An encyclopedia* (pp. 679–684). Grand Rapids, MI: Eerdmans.

Copeland, M. S. (2002). Body, representation, and black religious discourse. In L. E. Donaldson and P.-L. Kwok (Eds.), *Postcolonialism, feminism, and religious discourse* (pp. 180–198). New York: Routledge.

Davis, E. F. (2009). *Scripture, culture, and agriculture: An agrarian reading of the Bible.* New York: Cambridge University Press.

Dillard, A. (1994). *The Annie Dillard reader.* New York: Harper Collins.

Freyfogle, E. T. (Ed.) (2001) *The new agrarianism: Land, culture, and the community of life.* Washington, DC: Island Press.

Herdt, J. (2009). Christian humility, courtly civility, and the code of the streets. *Modern Theology, 25,* 541–561.

Hume, D. (1976). *An inquiry concerning the principles of morals.* Indianapolis: Bobbs-Merrill.

Jackson, W. (1996). Mattfield Green. In W. Vitek and W. Jackson (Eds.), *Rooted in the land: Essays on community and place* (pp. 95–103). New Haven, CT: Yale University Press.

Jantzen, G. (1995). *Power, gender, and Christian mysticism.* Cambridge: Cambridge University Press.

Kalvin, J. (1999). *Women breaking boundaries: A Grail journal, 1940–1995.* Albany: State University of New York Press.

Lusk, J. (2013). *The food police: A well-fed manifesto about the politics of your plate.* New York: Crown Forum.

Rist, J. (1994). *Augustine: Ancient thought baptized.* New York: Cambridge University Press.

Saiving, V. (1979). The human situation: A feminine view. In C. Christ and J. Plaskow (Eds.), *Womanspirit rising: A feminist reader in religion* (pp. 25–42). San Francisco: Harper and Row.

Sayre, L., and Clark., S. (Eds.) (2011). *Fields of learning: The student farm movement in North America*. Lexington: University Press of Kentucky.

Schwehn, M. R. (1993). *Exiles from Eden: Religion and the academic vocation in America*. New York: Oxford.

Stewart, C. (1998). *Prayer and community: The Benedictine tradition*. Maryknoll, NY: Orbis.

Voss Roberts, M. (2009). Retrieving humility: Rhetoric, authority, and divinization in Mechthild of Magdeburg. *Feminist Theology, 18*(1), 50–73.

Ward, B. (Ed.). (1975). *The sayings of the desert fathers*. Kalamazoo, MI: Cistercian Publications.

Whitman, W. (1881). *Leaves of grass*. Boston: James Osgood and Company.

Wirzba, N. (Ed.) (2003a). *The essential agrarian reader: The future of culture, community, and the land*. Lexington: University Press of Kentucky.

Wirzba, N. (2003b). *The paradise of God: Renewing religion in an ecological age*. New York: Oxford.

Wirzba, N. (2007). The dark night of the soil: An agrarian approach to mystical life. *Christianity and Literature, 56*, 253–274.

Wirzba, N. (2008). The touch of humility: An invitation to creatureliness. *Modern Theology, 24*, 225–244.

JECB 18:1 (2014): 41–59   1366-5456

Anne Lumb
Prioritizing Children's Spirituality in the Context of Church of England Schools: Understanding the Tensions

In the UK, inspectors are asked to judge how far schools support children's spiritual development. Church schools are subject to the differing expectations of a dual inspection system which introduces a tension between the Ofsted (Office for Standards in Education) prioritization of control and performativity and the SIAMS (Statutory Inspection of Anglican and Methodist Schools) prioritization of creativity and spirituality. This paper derives from a year-long study in a Church of England Primary School where meeting the requirements of these inspection systems to maintain high academic standards and provide space for children to explore spirituality created tensions and complexities. The paper presents a Bernsteinian analysis of the school's learning environment which elucidates the tensions within which headteachers and their staff operate and indicates the kind of support that church school leaders require if they are to respond to the demands of this 'double tension'.

Key words: children's spirituality, church schools, school inspection, spiritual space, pedagogy and performativity, Bersteinian analysis

In England, the Church's involvement in education pre-dates that of the state. However, with the advent of state education for all, Church of England schools became an integral part of the state system. The Church of England is now the largest single provider of schools in England. Since the 1944 Education Act all schools have been required to provide opportunities for children's spiritual development. This article examines the tensions this generates in Church of England schools, beginning with an examination of the impact of recent policy on school inspection, followed by the report of a case study conducted by the author in one school.

Church schools are inspected every three to five years through the Statutory Inspection of Anglican and Methodist Schools or SIAMS (The National Society, 2012) which focuses on the ways in which church schools are fulfilling the Church's aspiration that they should be both distinctively Christian and inclusive of all faiths and none (Dearing, 2001). In common with other state-funded schools, they are also inspected through the national school inspection system administered by the Office for Standards in Education (Ofsted, 2011b) where there is an emphasis on the examination of performance data to ensure that pupils are achieving appropriate levels of progress. This means that church schools are subject to the differing expectations of a dual inspection system.

This paper explores some of the tensions created for church schools by this dual inspection system, particularly where schools are seeking to create space for children to explore spirituality. The paper takes as its starting point the view that both academic standards and spiritual education are central to the mission of church schools. It posits that there is a 'double tension' faced by church schools and considers how best to support them in balancing the tensions of the high stakes environment created by accountability to both Ofsted and SIAMS where headteachers are vulnerable to the repercussions of an adverse inspection. The empirical research reported in this paper is derived from a year-long ethnographic study of the spiritual dimension of one church primary school which has achieved outstanding grades for both Ofsted and SIAMS inspections.

Inspecting Spirituality in the Church School Context

According to Dearing (2001), the purpose of Church of England schools is 'not simply to provide the basic education needed for human dignity' but to offer 'a spiritual dimension to the lives of young people, within the traditions of the Church of England, in an increasingly secular world' (p. 3). This emphasis on the spiritual dimension of life is reiterated in the Chadwick Report of 2012 (Chadwick, 2012), where it is said that church school distinctiveness 'must include a wholehearted commitment to putting faith and spiritual development at the heart of the curriculum and ensuring that a Christian ethos permeates the whole educational experience' (p. 3). Therefore, within a church school there is an expectation that discourse will be strongly framed within the Christian tradition, including an expectation that questions of faith (and therefore doubt) and doctrine will be opened up and explored within the curriculum.

Since the earliest days of Ofsted inspections in 1992, spirituality has featured in varying degrees within the inspection framework. Gilliat (1996) argues that 'spiritual development is a whole-school and whole-curriculum issue' (p. 171), an aspiration that was reiterated in the Ofsted Framework of 2011 (Ofsted, 2011a), where spiritual, moral, social, and cultural development was included as one of its seven judgements of quality for pupil outcomes (p. 14). Inspectors were to evaluate '[p]upils' development of personal insight and purpose, and their understanding of society's shared and agreed values' (p.28). The guidance issued to Ofsted inspectors in January 2012 (Ofsted, 2012) includes the requirement to report on 'indicators of spiritual development' such as beliefs (religious or otherwise); learning about self, others, and the world (including the intangible); use of imagination and creativity; and willingness to reflect (p. 23).

The SIAMS framework provides church schools with criteria by which schools self-evaluate their provision (including opportunities for exploring spirituality) and specialist inspectors judge and validate or challenge those evaluations. Here there is an emphasis on the provision of opportunities for pupils to 'engage in high quality experiences that develop a personal spirituality' (The National Society, 2012, p. 7) which goes beyond just providing high quality Religious Education. The award of the 'Outstanding' grade for the Christian character of the school requires 'a highly developed interpretation of spirituality shared across the school community' which will be evidenced by pupils who are 'passionate and confident to express their thoughts and views in considerable depth through a rich variety of styles and media' (p. 7).

Church schools are, therefore, expected to meet two different sets of inspection criteria. My argument in this paper is that these different demands create particular tensions within church schools where serious attempts are made to meet the requirement to achieve academically according to Ofsted criteria whilst also creating 'space' for the spiritual in order to meet the stringent requirements of SIAMS on spirituality. This tension is heightened by the emphasis in the Ofsted criteria on providing evidence of effective learning and placing less emphasis on spirituality.

Research by Troman, Jeffrey, and Raggl (2007, pp. 549–572) indicates that schools, caught in the high stakes accountability systems that currently operate in England and Wales, focus particularly on the collection of measureable data. Similarly Ball (2003) demonstrates the ways in which, in order to do well in these measurable terms, schools adopt forms of performativity that reflect the need to do well in inspections rather than pursue their own deep-seated beliefs about teaching. Ball discusses the effects of this performativity on the 'soul' of teachers who lose the sense of the authenticity of their work and professional identity. Teachers themselves become 'ontologically insecure: unsure whether we are doing enough, doing the right thing, doing as much as others, or as well as others, constantly looking to improve, to be better, to be excellent' (p. 220).

Ontologically insecure school environments, staffed by teachers who feel pressured into performative behaviours to achieve outstanding results, are probably not ideal sites for the development of children's spirituality. Research by Bryan and Revell (2011) with student religious education teachers indicated that this group 'felt that an explicit articulation of their faith was inappropriate within the performative context of school' (p. 413). According to Bryan and Revell, the 'organic relationship' which exists between the technical act of teaching (meeting externally determined outcomes) and 'the disposition that informs *praxis*' (where 'teaching' as described by Aristotle 'is transformed from a technical act, to 'education' which is practice located within the values of a given community') is 'at the heart of the tension between performativity and faith in the contemporary context' (p. 408).

Those committed to church schools would want them to achieve all-round academic excellence within the state system, as well as excellence in spiritual education; 'The drive for excellence and effectiveness in Church schools is paramount, but not merely because the Government says so. The enabling of every child to flourish in their potential as a child of God, is a sign and expression of the Kingdom and is at the heart of the Church's distinctive mission' (Chadwick, 2012, p. 3). But, as Green (2009) comments, the emphasis of governmental and parental concern has been with academic standards such that research has focused 'on studying the impact of schools with a Christian ethos on attainment, rather than their spiritual impact' (p. 83).

Defining Children's Spirituality in the Church School Context

An appropriate understanding of the term 'children's spirituality' is required if church schools are to respond positively to the view that spiritual education, as well as academic excellence, is central to their mission. In her review of research on the impact of schools with a Christian ethos, Green (2009) drew attention to the fact that researchers and schools lacked a shared language with which to discuss the nature, purpose, and impact of distinctively Christian education. This was, she continued, further complicated by the lack of agreed definitions for terms such as 'spirituality' and 'Christian ethos' (p. 79).

Definitions of spirituality which emphasize its 'everydayness' in the lives of children are exemplified in the research of both McCreery and Nye. In her investigation into the beliefs of four- and five-year-olds about the world in which they live, McCreery (1996) looked for ways in which we can know when we are developing the spiritual. She asks, what represents the 'ultimate' in children's lives? What questions do they ask about the world? What meaning do they find in life? In her research she attempts to discover *their* questions by giving them situations arising from familiar events and asking the children to identify the questions. For young children, she maintains, there is no need for artificial spiritual activities since everything around them is 'life'. In painting and drawing, for example, children are beginning their encounters and responses with themselves, other people, and the world around them. For McCreery, the spiritual is in the everyday; it is to do with living and is not specifically related to religion. These encounters and responses are important elements in a child's development (pp. 197–198).

Nye (2009) draws upon her experience as a psychologist, as well as an expert in children's spirituality, to offer three definitions of children's spirituality. One of these definitions takes an evidence-based approach using Nye's own research to define spirituality through the child's capacity for 'relational consciousness'. This 'relational consciousness', Nye argues,

45

exemplifies the view that '[i]n childhood, spirituality is especially about being attracted towards "being in relation", *responding to a call to relate* to more than "just me"—i.e. to others, to God, to creation or to an inner sense of Self. This encounter with transcendence can happen in specific experiences or moments, as well as through imaginative or reflective activity (thoughts and meaning making)' (p. 6).

Nye attempts to offer a definition of spirituality which is as inclusive as possible of the experiences of children, ensuring that it is not only experiences that can be recalled and talked about that are considered 'spiritual', but that all their imaginings, questionings, views, play, and ideas may be considered when gathering evidence of children's spirituality (Nye, 2009, p. 7).

Hull (2002) provides a useful framework within which to consider the relationship between spirituality, religion, and faith. According to Hull's argument, these three concepts can be viewed as three concentric circles—the largest on the outside being spirituality, the middle ring being religion and the inner circle being faith. Hull rejects the idea that the spiritual is a separable part of the human. He regards the spiritual, moral, and cultural references in the education legislation as 'aspects or dimensions of the human rather than as parts or sections'. In Hull's view, '[T]he spiritual is the whole of the human considered from a certain point of view, that of personhood continually transcending itself. So the spiritual refers to the achievement of human being. The spiritual process is the same as the process of humanisation' (p. 172). According to Hull, therefore, the cultural, mental, social and spiritual all refer to those aspects of being human which lift us above the biological. Thus Hull concludes that the biological, like the world of nature, has spiritual potential.

The views of these scholars were particularly pertinent within the context of the case study school. The headteacher's approach to exploring spirituality through literacy activities was influenced by Hull's definition of spirituality and the creation of an environment where spirituality could be explored within the life of the school resonated with the 'everydayness' of McCreery's spirituality and the emphasis on relationships highlighted by Nye.

The Case Study

The central purpose of my research was to develop an understanding of the spiritual dimension of a Church of England primary school and the ways in which spirituality is developed and nurtured in this context. There was a focus on the introduction of Philosophy for Children (P4C—the community of enquiry approach to learning developed by Matthew Lipman in the United States) and its impact on pupils' spiritual development.

This ethnographic study took place at St Saviour's Church of England Primary School. The school and all participants have been anonymised. The school has 230 pupils and serves three villages approximately ten miles from a large Midlands city. Pupils enter the school with levels of attainment generally above those expected for children of this age. Many are from socially and economically advantaged backgrounds. The proportion of children who have learning difficulties is below average, and only two pupils have a statement of special educational need. The percentage of pupils from minority ethnic backgrounds is lower than the national average, and all pupils speak English as their first additional language. The school has strong links with the parish church and the Anglican Diocese to which it belongs.

Access to the school was gained through my professional contacts with the headteacher and staff in my role as Diocesan Schools Adviser. The dual roles of adviser and researcher created ethical challenges which were overcome by having open discussions with staff, ensuring respondent validation of data and anonymizing the site. Data were collected between February 2010 and July 2011. For three terms during this period I visited the school weekly to facilitate P4C (see above) sessions with a class of 8- to 9-year-olds. Interviews were conducted with the headteacher, vicar, teaching staff, and pupils. Curriculum documents, school self-evaluation, and inspection reports were analysed. General observation, informal conversation, and photographic evidence also contributed to the data.

The data were coded thematically and Bernstein's pedagogical theories were used as the theoretical lens through which to analyse the data. Bernstein (1996) developed a series of models to describe the 'organisational, discursive and transmission practices' in 'all pedagogical agencies', including schools (p. 3). The analysis focused on his ideas around the framing and control of teaching discourses, the tensions between horizontal and vertical discourses, and the competence versus performance approach to pedagogy. An ethnographic approach was taken towards this study since the aim was to illuminate the issues through an in-depth single case study.

Defining Spirituality at St Saviour's

Written documentation indicated that staff had worked to define spirituality at St Saviour's. The school's self-evaluation document (the *Toolkit*) reported the belief that each person was created in God's image 'but with an understanding that this is about the gift of "spirit", in terms of spirituality that defines who we are and who we belong to.' The *Toolkit* also recorded that spiritual, moral, social, and cultural development (SMSC) were at the heart of the school's 'personality' since it was the foundation they built on and the 'spirit' that drove them: 'It has the potential to take us from the ordinary to the extra-ordinary and is something exemplified not by any one thing, but by the school itself.'

The headteacher, Mr Middleton, stated in an interview (September 10, 2010) that there was '[A] clear definition of spirituality [which] is at the heart of who we are.' This was reflected in the school's self-evaluation *Toolkit* which clearly articulated a sense of the school as a community in which spirituality was at the core of its meaning and purpose:

> St Saviour's is a community that genuinely believes in the power of spirit, both in terms of the school's personality and the spirituality which is at its heart, spirituality which sees itself fundamentally as about who we are and who we can become and which is defined within the special God given, Christ defined, bonds we share with those who are most precious to us—here, if anywhere, is the awe and wonder (the **W**orld of **W**onder factor) of [St Saviour's] Church of England Primary School.

Mr Middleton used Hull's definition of spirituality as a stimulus to experiment with 'the concept of challenging children to write using "emotional and spiritual language"' (paper written by the headteacher, *Extending the 'Gifted' Writer*, p. 1). He claimed that the use of such language 'encouraged pupils to tap into their deeper feelings' and release the spiritual potential referred to in Hull's account. He also associated spirituality with the development of an understanding of 'who we are at our deepest level' and our relationships with those who mean the most to us (headteacher interview, September 10, 2010), reflecting Nye's definition of spirituality expressed through 'relational consciousness' and the 'everydayness' of McCreery's view on spirituality.

Creating Space for Spirituality

Having a clearly articulated working definition of spirituality led to certain outcomes, in particular:

1. As a church school, collective worship and Religious Education (RE) occupied a central position in the everyday life of the school. Staff viewed collective worship as an important time for encouraging children's spiritual development. Mrs Jones (Y4 teacher) commented (interview, January 27, 2011) that the spiritual dimension of education 'links into collective worship' while Mr Wood (deputy head) stated (interview, April 6, 2011) that spiritual development was encouraged 'mainly through collective worship'. During interviews some of the children spoke about assemblies providing opportunities for thinking time and for asking questions. Sometimes these questions could be asked out loud within the worship time, at other times the children asked questions in their own minds about the story they had listened to. Mrs Scott (Year 3 teacher and RE co-ordinator) spoke in an interview (March 10, 2011) of the importance of developing thinking skills throughout the school. She considered that there were identifiable thinking spaces in the curriculum related specifically to RE and spiritual development. She gave examples of Year 1 pupils who would devise questions to ask God, Year 3 did an activity with colours which included opportunity to think about God, and Year 6 wrote poetry with a spiritual dimension. Pupils were expected to progress not only in their thinking skills but also in their ability to express spiritual ideas and feelings. These formal and informal settings provided opportunities

for the 'everyday spirituality' explored in the research of Nye and McCreery.

2. Within the curriculum a stepped approach to learning ensured that pupils gained the basics of language and literacy before being given access to specific opportunities to engage with spirituality in creative writing activities. Although the headteacher acknowledged the importance of developing literacy skills (field note, April 15, 2010), he also noted that the literacy should go further. He was keen to encourage self-belief and confidence in all pupils and challenged all the children to extend their thinking and writing. He was using creative writing to improve the pupils' SATs (Standard Attainment Tests taken at age 10–11) levels, but for him the real 'driver' was the development of spirituality and the use of spiritual and emotional language. In his view imagery and symbolism needed to be developed in order to move on to a more 'spiritual' level.

3. The introduction of P4C provided space for children to engage in a community of enquiry where potentially spiritual questions could be explored by all children regardless of their ability to express their ideas in writing. Mrs Jones (Class 4 teacher involved in P4C sessions), in an interview (January 20, 2011), expressed the view that the spiritual dimension of education could be enhanced by P4C and that she had become more interested in spirituality herself since being involved in P4C sessions. She had observed the children expressing 'big' questions in general conversation, using skills she had not seen in this age group before: '[I]t's affecting the way they think.' She had also noticed that 'less academic' children were 'coming out with "strong" thoughts' and she had seen different aspects to the children which she may not have seen otherwise. These outcomes were reflected in the outstanding inspection grades achieved by the school in both Ofsted and SIAMS.

Tensions in the Language of Pedagogy

The pedagogy at St Saviour's ensured that skills were acquired through a step-on-step approach which reflected Bernstein's (2000) performance model of pedagogic practice. The performance model emphasizes what the learner cannot do or does not know. The learner is therefore required to receive the 'correct' text from the transmitter or teacher. The sense of deficit places emphasis on the text to be acquired and on the transmitter of this knowledge to create an ordered performance model whereby the learner cannot proceed to 'higher' stages of learning until the preliminary steps of appropriate knowledge gained or skills acquired are in place (p. 57). The philosophy at St Saviour's meant that literacy skills were required before the children were expected to be able to express their thoughts, ideas, and emotions through writing; the building blocks of learning were expected to be in place before a higher spiritual awareness could be expressed. Learners were taught the skills and knowledge they did not know, according to their performance in relation to the levels prescribed by the National Curriculum. These approaches to the teaching of writing and the performance of an event followed the stages identified by Piaget where children first learned skills (how to 'do') in an individualistic, concrete way before they were enabled to express 'spiritual' ideas. This performance model revealed a desire for high attainment and outcomes which led to a controlling of the pedagogy and crucially meant that space within the curriculum for spiritual development for children with low level literacy skills was limited.

However, practice at St Saviour's also embraced Bernstein's competence model where the emphasis is placed on empowerment—what you can do or know. These are 'practical accomplishments' which are creative and 'tacitly acquired in informal interactions' (Bernstein, 2000, p. 4). Within the competence model (in contrast to the performance model) learners discover what they already know and think and are provided with the opportunity to develop this knowledge further. This approach to learning was illustrated at St Saviour's through the introduction of Philosophy for Children (P4C) where the children (and their teacher) explored a stimulus together by expressing their initial ideas to each other, trying out new ideas with each other, and thereby learning together. The community of enquiry approach employed within P4C reflected the view of Vygotsky (1986) that children learn first in community. Their learning

51

was then internalized and they proceeded to more individualized forms of learning (p. 36). The competence model thus illustrates the desire which also existed in the school whereby all children could be allowed space to grow and develop spiritually through a freeing up of the pedagogy.

These contrasting theories of learning introduced a distinctive layer in the tensions being explored in this paper. The individualistic approach to learning encouraged by the performance model enabled children to develop and express a deep awareness of self. One of the central concepts articulated by the headteacher was that children should be given opportunities to discover who they are 'at their deepest level' and that in making such discoveries they should also be given opportunities to communicate what they found through writing. Alongside this individualistic approach to learning was the social model of learning demonstrated through competence pedagogy where children (and teachers) learned alongside one another, exploring concepts and ideas together. The emphasis was on talking and listening, on trying out ideas rather than on producing a written piece. At the end of a P4C session all participants in the discussion were given an opportunity to speak their 'final thoughts' on the original question under discussion. Each child expressed their ideas and questions in a safe environment knowing those ideas were being valued and listened to.

The language for talking about their collective vision at St Saviour's had been established by the headteacher, who was remarkably effective in using language to communicate to staff and pupils and in encouraging them to use the language he had established. Aphorisms, such as 'TAKE CARE', permeated the discourse of the school. The leadership of Mr Middleton provided a clearly articulated notion of spirituality and a certainty of approach which may be termed the 'St Saviour's way'. Exploring 'who we are at our deepest level' was, according to the headteacher, the core principle of the school and was partly delivered through a 'take care' philosophy. Mr Middleton claimed that the more we understand who we are and who others are through our relationships and our empathy with one another, the more chance we have of developing spiritually. He continued:

> I mean spirituality for us is about who we are at our deepest level
> and that sense of feeling we have for those who are most important
> to us. . . . Actually when we take care of each other, we take care
> of the world we give ourselves the opportunity to find more of

that and become closer to people and things that are important and of course in a church school context, closer to God if that's where you choose to go but that's not our purpose, that's just a question we might ask, another level of possibility that we might offer to a child. (headteacher interview, September 10, 2010)

An interpretation could be that the headteacher is attempting to resolve the tension between operating within the controlled framework of a Christian ethos (defined by the church and regulated by SIAMS inspections where there are specific criteria to meet) and providing opportunities to explore questions of faith and, therefore, doubt, enabling the church school to 'Nourish those of the faith; Encourage those of other faiths; Challenge those who have no faith' (Dearing, 2001, p. 4).

Other tensions were articulated in the school's documentation. For example, in the school's *Active Curriculum* document the headteacher articulated that his aim was to 'liberate the creative heart of the school' in a 'well considered, disciplined and qualitative way'; which raises the question, can creativity always be 'liberated' in a 'disciplined way'? There was a calm and courteous atmosphere within the school, but the definition of creativity on which this atmosphere was based did not sit easily with definitions of spirituality which ask deep and unsettling questions that do not always produce neat, disciplined answers. There was a contrast here between the headteacher's drive to control the pedagogy (thereby maintaining the high levels of performativity demanded by Ofsted) and his desire to allow the freedom to explore spirituality when staff were given permission to 'stop and be creative' (reflecting the creativity and spirituality prioritized by SIAMS).

According to Bernstein (2000), 'control' establishes the language to be used whilst 'power' establishes who speaks to whom. Control, Bernstein claims, establishes 'different forms of communication appropriate to different categories' (p. 5). Control determines the type of language that can be used and can determine both what is reproduced and what may change. Teachers and teaching assistants were aware of the aphorisms or 'memorable statements' that were integral to the pedagogical language of the school and were expected to provide learning experiences which incorporated the values expressed in them. There was a 'St Saviour's way' of doing things which was reflected in this language and provided a unifying force for the whole school community. The key statement about the school, according to the headteacher, was that 'we are a "take care" school'. This, he claimed, was understandable (on the surface) by anybody; it enabled teachers to use a common language and children to 'begin to articulate what the school stands for'; 'It's something that parents can understand, that governors can understand, that the community can share in and also it's the core of the value system we share with the church . . . and therefore we believe that if you went to the children and asked them what the school stood for most of them would be able to tell you it's a 'take care' school and know something about what that meant' (headteacher interview, September 10, 2010). This claim was borne out during the fieldwork period; when asked during a collective worship time, 'What makes this school?' one of the answers given by the children was, 'We take care' (field note, July 5, 2011). The language used within the curriculum and reflected throughout the life of the school created the correct 'St Saviour's' response from the child, displaying the tension inherent in the use of language which implies both an individualistic approach to producing and being the best they could be whilst providing opportunities for children to take part in a learning community.

Complexity of Effect

This analysis of the language and curriculum of the school revealed both positive and negative effects on the potential to create spiritual spaces and to encourage the spiritual nurture and development of the children. This generated a level of complexity which is illustrated by the leadership style of the headteacher. His clear definition of spirituality ensured that both staff and pupils knew that matters of faith and spirituality could be discussed openly and that the creation of space for spirituality within the school day was an expectation and available to all members of the school community. However, the headteacher's use of the language of 'permission' in speaking of this space creation also suggested an element of deficit and a desire to control where the 'gaps' for spirituality would be located and made manifest each day. There was 'permission' to create space despite the climate of performativity created by Ofsted demands which might be seen as militating against this. However, the space was still within the boundaries set by the headteacher. This control of language appeared to be working effectively in this context but could be at odds with the notion that spirituality is concerned with developing a personal language and that very tight control of language development might hinder the potential for spiritual development.

This complexity was further illustrated by examples of both control and autonomy within the school. For example, the school provided a 'prayer wall' that gave a structure which was inclusive since any child who wished to could write a prayer on a sticky note and display it. This teaching structure allowed openness in a public display which contrasted with the approach of allowing only the more able children to access certain activities designed to explore specific aspects of spirituality. Similarly, the inclusive nature of P4C sessions contrasted with the spirituality-related activities reserved for older or more able children.

The key aphorism 'take care' itself provides an illustration of this complexity operating at different levels within the school community. The phrase 'take care' has several different connotations—from showing love and care for others, yourself, and the environment to producing your best work, to a warning to 'be careful' in a place of danger. It could be understood at different levels by all members of the school community since it contained layers of meaning and could allow individuals to make up their own layers of meaning, freeing up thinking and playing with language. By building on the simple concept of 'take care', children could become better equipped to cope with the more abstract layers of meaning later.

The stepped approach to literacy and learning discussed above contrasted with the encouragement for teachers and pupils to take risks in being creative. Clear definitions and 'right answers' indicated a control of discourse patterns which were both positive and negative in their effect. Spaces for spirituality were created, along with opportunities to create meaning through ambiguity and layered meaning (as in the aphorisms noted above); yet conversely, such 'right answers' could prevent individuals thinking for themselves, simply repeating taught definitions. The risk-averse culture of Ofsted (with its emphasis on providing correct answers) had created the need to ensure a consistency of approach to teaching and learning (creating order, 'taking care'), which could be at odds with the spaces created to facilitate the somewhat risky task of exploring the mystery and meaning of life. Creativity and spirituality involve 'risk' since mystery is at the heart of existence. At such points there are not necessarily right or final answers, in contrast to the demands of performing for Ofsted when often the search is for the right answer to a question and one of the unwritten rules of the classroom is that the pupil's task 'in teacher-pupil discourse is to find the "right" answer ("guess what I'm thinking")' (Alexander, 2000 pp. 382–383) and avoid taking the risk of providing the 'wrong' answer.

It could be argued, therefore, that St Saviour's school was operating within the 'culture of grace' in which, Worsley (2013) claims, Christians 'can fulfil and even go beyond Ofsted' since 'in many ways, Christ lived in an "Ofsted culture" where he had to abide by the terms of the law, but had some things to say about the application of the law. He healed on a Sabbath, his disciples picked and ate grain on a Sabbath. Yet Jesus claimed he had not come to abolish the law but to fulfil it' (p. 5). It is in such a context that questions of meaning and purpose can be explored.

Conclusion

The reality in which Anglican church school headteachers operate is that of a highly performative culture in which the dual system of inspection has an implicit hierarchy with Ofsted above SIAMS in status; where to be outstanding requires high levels of academic achievement alongside a commitment to developing children's spirituality. The development of a climate in which teachers and children know that there is the kind of time and space available to explore spirituality and reflect on learning experiences requires the establishment of leadership patterns that welcome and encourage thinking space within the curriculum as part of the everyday fabric of the school. There is, therefore, a need for church school leaders to be provided with opportunities to develop a reflective theology that will inform both their thinking and their practice. Brown (2013) states that there is a constant challenge to the Church of England's Board of Education and the National Society 'to express its mission in clear theological terms and to present headteachers with a clear and accessible theology' (p. 157). Elbourne (2013, p. 248) attempts to 'explore more deeply what might be the characteristic essence of being a church school in the current situation' using the concepts of 'Rootedness, Belonging and Narrative' to go beyond the mantra of 'distinctiveness' and 'inclusivity' highlighted by Dearing (2001).

Hart (2003) writes of the importance of meeting with others to discuss 'the spiritual' since '[h]onest and open conversation about the meaning of life and the nature of the spirit can be like fresh air' (pp. 222, 229). Dioceses should look at ways of extending their provision of such opportunities for church school leaders and their staff to engage in recognizing and developing spiritual awareness, to participate in opportunities for reflection within training events, and to take part in spiritual 'retreat'.

Dioceses and the National Society, therefore, have a vital role to play in ensuring that teachers and leaders in Anglican church schools have opportunities to engage with their own spirituality; to develop a reflective theology which provides a greater understanding of the particular role that a church school can have in nurturing children's spirituality; to develop a pedagogy which encourages a 'community of enquiry' as part of its strategy; and to ensure that more classrooms become 'safe spaces' in which children can explore the questions that are so important to them.

If Christian educationalists are to support headteachers in discovering a Christian way of providing the best education for the children in their care, the tensions that result from attempting to produce the outcomes expected by the dual inspection process whilst fulfilling the desire to explore spirituality need to be acknowledged. Further unravelling is required in order to see the tensions being played out in the curriculum. For example, the freedom to doubt and explore alongside presenting the teachings of a particular religion; the impact on the role of the headteacher in managing the tensions between accountability and ensuring that the school community reflects openness and Christian teaching; and acknowledging where power lies in the control of language and giving children control as they have opportunities to explore their own thoughts and ideas. Consideration needs to be given to exploring how church schools can experience these risks and tensions whilst discovering ways of embedding spirituality at classroom level.

References

Alexander, R. (2000). *Culture and pedagogy*. Oxford: Blackwell.

Ball, S.J. (2003). The teacher's soul and the terrors of performativity. *Journal of Education Policy, 18*(2), 215–228.

Bernstein, B. (2000). *Pedagogy, symbolic control and identity*. Lanham, MD: Rowman & Littlefield.

Brown, A. (2013). The church schools as "safe" school. In H. Worsley (Ed.), *Anglican church school education* (pp.151–166). London: Bloomsbury.

Bryan, H., & Revell, L. (2011) Performativity, faith and professional identity: Student religious education teachers and the ambiguities of objectivity. *British Journal of Educational Studies, 59*(4), 403–419.

Chadwick, P. (2012). *The church school of the future review.* London: Archbishop's Council Education Division.

Dearing, R. (2001). *The way ahead: Church of England schools in the new millenium.* London: Church House Publishing.

Elbourne, T. (2013). Church school identity beyond the Dearing era. In H. Worsley (Ed.), *Anglican church school education* (pp. 239–254). London: Bloomsbury.

Gilliat, P. (1996). Spiritual education and public policy 1944–1994. In R. Best (Ed.), *Education, spirituality and the whole child* (pp. 161–172). London: Cassell.

Green, E. (2009). *Mapping the field: A review of the current research evidence on the impact of schools with a Christian ethos.* London: Theos.

Hart, T. (2003). *The secret spiritual world of children.* Novato, CA: New World Library.

Hart, T. (2006). Spiritual experiences and capacities of children and youth. In E. Roehkepartain et al. (Eds.), *The handbook of spiritual development in childhood and adolescence* (pp. 163–177). Thousand Oaks, CA: Sage Publications.

Hull, J. M. (2002). Spiritual development: Interpretations and applications. *British Journal of Religious Education, 24*(3), 171–182.

McCreery, E. (1996). Talking to young children about things spiritual. In R. Best (Ed), *Education, spirituality and the whole child* (pp. 197–205). London: Cassell.

Nye, R. (2009). *Children's spirituality: What is it and why it matters.* London: Church House Publishing.

Office for Standards in Education. (2011a). *The evaluation schedule for schools.* London: HMSO.

Office for Standards in Education. (2011b). *The framework for school inspection.* London: HMSO.

Office for Standards in Education. (2012). *Subsidiary guidance: Supporting the inspection of maintained schools and academies from January 2012.* London: HMSO.

The National Society. (2012). *The evaluation schedule for the statutory inspection of Anglican and Methodist schools.* London: National Society.

Troman, G., Jeffrey, B., & Raggl, A. (2007). Creativity and performativity policies in primary school cultures. *Journal of Education Policy, 22*(5), 549–572.

Vygotsky, L. (1986). *Thought and language*. Cambridge, MA: The MIT Press.

Worsley, H. (2013.) *What motivates Christian education practitioners*. Nottingham, UK: The Stapleford Centre. Retrieved from http://www.stapleford-centre.org/conferences/what-motivates-christian-education-practitioners.

JECB 18:1 (2014): 61–75   1366-5456

Ros Stuart-Buttle

Interrupting Adult Learning through Online Pedagogy

This paper considers online pedagogy in relation to Christian adult learning and asks how this might be interpreted by theological educators. The online community of inquiry is proposed as one recognized pedagogical approach and illustrated by reference to a continuing professional development programme for online adult learners across the church school sector in the UK. In seeking an online pedagogy that is also theologically informed, attention is given to Belgian theologian Lieven Boeve's work concerning a theology of interruption. Insights gained from this are considered alongside reflection from the author's experience as online educator. The paper concludes that online pedagogy can be interpreted as interruptive when influencing and shaping the online environment for adult theological learning.

Key words: online learning; online pedagogy; adult learning; theology of interruption; interruptive pedagogy

Introduction

Educators today ask how online technologies can be used to support an environment that enables learners to engage in meaningful learning. Online technologies facilitate contemporary teaching and learning as well as being media for human communication and expression. A convergence of online technologies delivers and supports a range of teaching and learning experiences (Holmes & Gardner, 2006). Initially dependent on text-based web conferencing, online learning increasingly features sophisticated and interactive digital media. In many formal educational settings, online courseware and communications are hosted within the infrastructure of a virtual learning environment. This means that long-standing assumptions about the relationship between time, place, pace, and physical presence in education are changing (Morgan-Klein & Osborne, 2007). This paper explores a theologically informed approach to the question of how these changes should be viewed in the context of adult theological education, drawing upon Lieven Boeve's theology of interruption.

Different approaches to online pedagogy influence the design, delivery, and quality of the learning experience. As teaching moves away from the physical or face-to-face classroom, some researchers suggest that a new pedagogy is needed. Proponents claim that online learning is pedagogically disruptive because it moves away from traditional patterns and towards new flexible, informal, and innovative teaching and learning approaches (Siemens, 2004; Downes, 2007; Kop, 2007; Meyer, 2010). However, other literature pays less attention to the idea of online pedagogical novelty, seeing instead that online learning depends upon a wide range of pedagogical practices that emerge from existing educational theories applied in the online environment according to the philosophy or infrastructure of the online educator. One pedagogical camp looks towards the objectivist view of knowledge and emphasises transmission of learning outcomes and course materials over more active learning processes (Weller, 2007). Knowledge is imparted from teacher (or computer) to learner through successful instructional design principles. This mode of online learning tends towards a sustaining or replication of existing instructional practices as pedagogy is transferred from face-to-face classroom practice into the online environment (Gulati, 2004). However, questions remain about the quality of learner experience this brings (Stephenson, 2001).

The discourse about online pedagogy is, however, more generally linked with the educational theories and principles of constructivism (Salmon, 2003; Morgan-Klein & Osborne, 2007; Mason & Rennie, 2008) that acknowledge the active role of the learner in constructing knowledge. These broadly state that views of the world are not objective or stable but change as learners reflect and build on past experiences, with new knowledge and understanding occurring in and through these active constructions. Dewey (1966), Vygotsky (1962), Brookfield (1986), and Bruner (1986) can be highlighted among those who have significantly influenced the constructivist field. From such theories, a more widely accepted understanding of online pedagogy has emerged which holds that active processes of dialogue, collaboration, and interaction are fundamental to learning. Online constructivist pedagogy seeks 'active meaning-making and interpretation of experience which is communal, collaborationalist and negotiable' (Carusi, 2003, p. 96). Gulati (2004) states that online pedagogy must reflect learning for real-life contexts with flexibility, collaboration, and openness among learning participants. Mason and Rennie (2008) favour 'an open-ended, negotiable approach which structures activities so that students have opportunities to collaboratively negotiate knowledge and to contextualize learning within an emergent situation' (p. 17). Lee (2010) succinctly summarizes constructivist pedagogy as learner-centred, context-rich, and experience-based.

This paper is concerned with online pedagogy in relation to adult learning in the context of theological education. In the field of adult learning, Freire (1972) is a key exponent of pedagogies that moved away from a 'banking' of programmed content towards more interactive and critical models of learning. Knowles (1980), in his theory of andragogy, considers the adult learner as possessing particular characteristics, needs, and resources that strongly influence the learning situation. Schön (1983) asserts a need for critical and reflective activity in order for adults to develop in their professional role. Mezirow (1991) sees how adult learners become autonomous thinkers through negotiating their own meaning systems (ideas, beliefs, values, experience) rather than uncritically acting on those of others. Such theories inform adult theological education which recognizes both exploration of doctrinal content and attention to shared human experience. Theological educators understand that critical dialogue and reflective activity help adult learners know their own starting points and embedded positions which, once recognized, can be challenged towards new or more meaningful theological frames of reference. Allowing space and creating opportunities for self-reflection and reflection-in-dialogue-with-others is an essential pedagogical principle. Opportunities to examine assumptions or question one's theological stance or faith identity can deepen an existing worldview or allow it to take on new meaning, especially when articulated in sustained critical conversation with others (De Bary, 2003). A pedagogy of adult theological learning based on conversation and dialogue, both inner and social, invites an appreciation of diversity and opens possibilities for healthy debate and creative thinking

(Stone & Durk, 2006). The development of critical openness, together with theological reflection, can afford a genuine search and readiness to act for personal and social change (Regan, 2002).

Christian educators hold a commitment to salvation history and gospel values. They also have the task of helping adult learners think critically about contemporary spiritual and moral issues, interpret them wisely, and forge relevant meaning, purpose, and values for today (Rossiter, 1999). The challenge not only is to present Christian tradition in rich and stimulating curriculum frameworks. It is to invite attention to cultural, personal, and professional contexts in relation to church teaching and tradition. Authentic learning seeks engagement with Christian doctrine in fresh approaches that encourage a critical learning process to help shape one's 'personal interpretative map for meaning-making' (D'Orsa, 2013, p. 76). This suggests a need for Christian educators to be open to new pedagogical approaches. But what might this look like for online adult learning? And what theological insights might illuminate online pedagogy?

Method

This paper is framed within an interpretative paradigm that draws on my professional experience in leading an online programme of adult theological learning over the past decade as well as on extensive case study research carried out among online theological educators and adult learners. It does not present research data or state findings, as these have been reported elsewhere (Stuart-Buttle, 2013). Instead, the paper offers an interpretation of online pedagogy that is also theologically informed. It shares some reflective insights about online pedagogy as a different educational space. This invites us to reflect on how people learn theology in contemporary situations.

References to adult online theological learning in the paper relate to a long-standing programme of continuing professional development for adults who are mostly (but not all) teachers working across the church school sector in the UK. A minority are involved in pastoral ministries or studying for personal faith development. The course is a national programme with a curriculum set by the Board of Studies of the Catholic Bishops' Conference of England and Wales but delivered through local diocesan centres and universities. It consists of eight components, with required teaching hours, fixed learning outcomes, and assessment criteria.[1] The online mode of programme study was proposed to the Bishops' Conference in 2001 and since 2004 has been accepted as a fully validated certification route. There is no requirement for campus attendance; instead, learners are invited to engage fully in the online environment. Online participants are attracted from across the UK, many of them citing reasons of flexibility of delivery and access that suits professional lives as well as enhanced opportunities for networking and collaboration. Since its inauguration, hundreds of adult learners have participated in this online programme to raise their levels of theological literacy and learn how to apply theological frameworks to professional practice and understanding of Christian faith.

Online Community of Inquiry

The online programme outlined above is broadly based upon the community of inquiry pedagogical model (Garrison et al., 2000). This model is widely recognized among online researchers and practitioners. It places online educators and learners as active participants in the learning process and invites collaborative-constructivist pedagogy, without losing focus on the cognitive aspects of teaching and learning. The online community of inquiry depends upon the interaction of three key elements: cognitive, social, and teaching presence. We briefly outline each in turn.

'Cognitive presence' refers to how online learners construct and confirm meaning. In order for this to occur, a context for critical thinking is needed that relates not just to individual internal learning processes but to the reciprocal relationship between learning contents and real life/work/faith experience. Online pedagogy, therefore, needs to encourage learners to interact with course materials which are purposefully designed to invite personal meaning and knowledge construction through shared inquiry and online discourse. This can be prompted through structured online discussions, reflective journaling, blogging, collaborative online activities, and informal/formal assessment tasks. These interactions are built into the pedagogical design in order to move beyond transmission of learning content or mere exchange of theological information. Instead, the pedagogical goal is to 'draw learners into a shared experience for the purposes of constructing and confirming deeper meaning' (Garrison, 2000, p. 95).

Social presence within the community of inquiry refers to how online learners interact with others in the online environment. They need to establish social relationships around common educational goals and find 'emotional expression, open communication, and group cohesion' (Garrison, 2000, p. 99). This is achieved when learners 'project their personal characteristics into the community, thereby presenting themselves to other participants as "real people"' who are able and willing to articulate feelings related to the educational experience (p. 89). Open and safe online communication can build mutual awareness, foster reflective peer responses, share values, and enhance community principles and ways of working together. This can be brought about in both formal and informal social interactions through peer discussion, live chat, personal e-mail and messaging, and video conferencing. However, it needs to be recognized that while fostering group cohesion and belonging is an important aspect of online pedagogy, it does present challenges. Online social presence is neither guaranteed nor automatically achieved since all human communication, including online mediated expression, carries a potential for misunderstanding and redundancies of meaning.

The third element in the community of inquiry is teaching presence, defined as 'the design, facilitation and direction of cognitive and social processes for the realization of personally meaningful and educationally worthwhile outcomes' (Swan et al., 2008, p. 1). The online educator is critical within this understanding of pedagogy. 'Appropriate cognitive and social presence, and ultimately, the establishment of a critical community of inquiry, is dependent upon the presence of a teacher' (Garrison et al., 2000, p. 96). Online teaching presence cannot be ignored, although the emerging discourse does recognize a changed role from the traditional instructor or academic expert to that of facilitator or learning guide. This can be construed in three ways. The online educator influences the pedagogical design in terms of how course materials, learning activities, and assessment practices are selected, organized, and presented, and also establishes course parameters and organizational guidelines. He or she also takes a lead role in supporting and encouraging the collaborative capabilities of learners to realize educational outcomes by helping them share meaning, identify agreement and disagreement, and reach consensus for knowledge exchange and understanding. This may include drawing in less active participants, giving acknowledgement to individual contributors, or directing/challenging/weaving the online discussion activity (Garrison et al., 2000, p. 101). The online educator exercises intellectual leadership and pedagogical expertise by sharing resources, diagnosing misconceptions, and giving feedback for learning. In summary, he or she operates within a pedagogy predicated on contact, communication, feedback, and flexibility (Brennan, 2003).

The online community of inquiry demonstrates one model for adult learning and has underpinned this author's online professional practice. Now we might ask how online pedagogy can be theologically informed. We turn to the work of Belgian theologian Lieven Boeve (2007, 2009a, 2009b, 2009c) who proposes a re-contextualization of Christian education in a postmodern cultural context. How might his theology of interruption inform an understanding and interpretation of online theological pedagogy?

Theology of Interruption

In recent times, theologians and educators have sought to invite dialogue with the postmodern world in order to bring the Christian narrative into the contemporary context. The idea of continuity holds that Christian faith must be in dialogue with contemporary culture and society in order to bridge or open new possibilities for Christian expression. However, critics hold a different reading of the Christian narrative, seeing discontinuity or rupture between faith and a secularized, pluralist, and de-traditionalized contemporary world. Such critique limits the possibilities of reciprocal dialogue by closing off Christian faith and tradition. According to Boeve, neither continuity nor discontinuity does justice to the essential link between God and salvation history. If the Christian worldview is closed from the contemporary context, then it is removed from present-day lived experience. On the other hand, if continuity is maintained too easily with the contemporary world, then there is a risk of Christian frames of reference being reduced to the private domain or immersed in a conflicting plurality of worldviews, which poses serious challenges concerning the identity, particularity, and truth claims of Christianity in a secularized and relativist world. So, how can Christian teaching and learning take on plausible and legitimate expression within the changing and challenging context of today?

It is here that Boeve offers a theological concept of interruption as a way for Christians to 'reconsider and reformulate the identity, credibility and relevance of their faith' (2009a. p. 4). A theology of interruption is a not a half-way house, lying mid-way between continuity and discontinuity. Nor it is capitulation, abandonment, or overly easy adaptation of faith to culture. Rather, Boeve proposes a theological model of interruption as a means to open up the Christian narrative to the 'otherness' of contemporary culture so that it thereby can be reconfigured or changed by new insight and incursion. The Christian narrative remains recognizably the same narrative, even if challenged in the process and shaped or enriched anew. This is what Boeve (2007) presents as theological interruption. It offers both dialogical method and imperative to engage Christian tradition with contemporary culture (p. 103).

Boeve (2009c) demonstrates that the Christian narrative has been and always is being interrupted by an encounter with otherness. The story of salvation is permeated by interruption, from a God who reveals himself through creation and the Scriptures, to the incarnational in-breaking of Jesus Christ into human history, whose very birth, death, and resurrection serve as the supreme model of interruption. So the Christian narrative is never closed but continually permeated by newness of encounter with the divine 'other'. The Christian story is always open to a new reality of God at work in the church, in the world, in personal living, and in those encountered through a plurality of worldviews, cultures, and situations. This interruption confronts our personal and communal narratives and is the place where God can become known and revealed. For Boeve, this invites a dynamic praxis of interruption which invites faithfulness to one's own particular narrative identity and tradition, at the same time as opening up to and respecting the other. This praxis moves beyond patterns of continuity or discontinuity to invite a theological re-imagining and re-articulation of the Christian gospel in the contemporary situation.

Online Pedagogy as Interruption

Boeve's theology of interruption suggests that while the core of the Christian narrative holds true, at the same time it must be open to fresh expression in contemporary cultural contexts in order to continue to speak to its own internal community and engage with the external world. Boeve does not relate a theology of interruption directly to online pedagogy or the practice of Christian education. Therefore, what insights might be gained from it? Rather than replicating a debate about whether online learning disrupts, transforms, or merely sustains pedagogy, a different approach for Christian educators is to consider how online pedagogy is interruptive in theological vision and for educational praxis. The remainder of the paper now takes up this discussion.

Learning viewed through a lens of interruption carries resonance for theological education. Each new learning situation invites continuity with tradition or what has gone before, at the same time as it opens up new possibilities. Authentic learning is never about reiterating a closed narrative but is rather about being open to new articulation. For learners themselves, this might mean acquiring new knowledge/understanding, transformed perspectives, or realization of personal insight/development. Stern (2013) points out that real learning always involves surprise. In doing so, he echoes the educational ideas of philosopher Martin Buber (2002), that learning is 'neither a routine repetition nor a lesson whose findings the teacher knows before he starts, but one which develops in mutual surprise' (p. 241). Approaching pedagogy through a lens of interruption takes us beyond seeing learning as technical exchange of information prompted by a need for objective understanding or as monologue that repeats or reinforces the status quo (ibid, p. 22). Instead, it opens up a sense of learning that allows the unexpected to interrupt the learner and/ or the learning process or situation.

The idea of interruption carries further relevance when traditional courses are moved into the online environment, as this gives theological educators an opportunity to re-think existing strategies and learning organization. In moving away from the traditional classroom framework, online pedagogy invites more open and personalized approaches to learning, available in synchronous/asynchronous mode with accessible and flexible 24/7 delivery. Learning opportunities are extended via online technologies for adults in their homes, schools, workplaces, parishes, or places of ministry. This encourages adult learners to engage in theological study, previously deemed irrelevant, inaccessible, or impossible for adult lifestyles challenged by family, work, ministry, and personal-social commitments. Geography and time are removed as defining characteristics of participation and interaction, creating new opportunities to take up faith study beyond the local parish, college, or catechism class. The scope and vision of Christian educational ministry is thus opened up by online possibilities. This has significance for the ownership of theology, formerly the preserve of the university, seminary, or specialist theologian. It suggests a different sort of theology, not derived from academics or church hierarchy but emerging from within the ordinary people of God (Astley, 2002; De Bary, 2003).

Online pedagogy determines course design and curriculum materials. Whereas a traditional course may depend on linear structures and hierarchical thinking to shape courseware and resources, online learning uses interactive hypertext materials. This allows selection of and access to learning contents according to personal order, choice, control, timing, and pace. The ability to download, add or annotate one's own or another's work, or extend a primary text or online posting beyond the boundary or meaning of the original author becomes possible. E-mail, discussion boards, blogs, wikis, social bookmarking, file-sharing, RSS feeds, Web search, instant messaging, social networking, virtual worlds, audio or video podcasts, or e-portfolios may feature in the learning design. Such technologies open up interruptive and unexpected dimensions as it is not always possible to anticipate or control how they are used in the service of learning. Learning may well take place beyond the scope or control of the online educator, especially when online discussion and peer collaborations occur behind more visible course structures (Huang, 2002).

Online pedagogy presents learning resources that invite user-generated content. This raises epistemological questions about the nature of knowledge, which many theological educators agree is more than mere online information exchange. Sajjadi (2008) sees a danger in online pedagogy taking religious knowledge and interpretation away from authoritative sources. This, he suggests, interrupts the authoritative nature of religious tradition and encourages the emergence of personalized knowledge spaces built through the agency of learners as co-authors of knowledge-construction and co-producers of meaning. We recognize instead a creative or interruptive tension for the online educator, whose task is to uphold the wisdom of Scripture and doctrinal tradition while, at the same time, encouraging communal inquiry, experiential-critical reflection, and peer communication according to the character, needs, hopes, fears, and experiences of adult learners themselves.

We saw earlier that the online community of inquiry holds cognitive, social, and teaching presence as key elements for collaborative rather than instrumental learning (Lewis, 2007). Increasingly, online educators recognize that effective online pedagogy depends upon successful relationships within an inquiring community (Downes, 2007; Garrison et al. 2000; Holmes & Gardner, 2006; Palloff & Pratt, 2007). This means that attention is needed for quality and depth of conversation, reciprocal exchange, negotiation of meaning, and the development of relationships to support learning and teaching (Ascough, 2007). Notions of Christian education rest strongly upon the centrality of human community and personal relationships (Dinges, 2006; Gresham, 2006). Palmer (1998) reminds us that education will only be truly transformative when it cherishes the human person who lies at the heart of the enterprise. This invites relationships in which we speak and listen, make claims on others, and become accountable to those around us. The cultivation of such learning communities of truth, Palmer argues, should be the goal of Christian education. Critics might question whether this is possible in the online environment and challenge the quality of human communication, identity, and relationships expressed there. However, research indicates that genuine relationships and enriching experiences of growing in faith exist among people who authentically share themselves, their learning, and their lives in the online environment (Hess, 2005; Campbell, 2005; Stuart-Buttle, 2013).

Online pedagogy affects the ways that learners think and communicate, theologically and educationally. It allows access to religious narrative and educational discourse in ways previously unknown. It presents new possibilities for belonging, communicating, relating, being present, and sharing faith with others. It brings about cognitive and affective learning when exchange of narratives takes place with mutual respect, trust, and a critical yet open and reflective spirit (Gresham, 2006; Zukowski, 2000). It is a missed opportunity if Christian educators fail to take notice of this new space for learning (Stuart-Buttle, 2011). Online pedagogy changes how people learn, and it prompts educational practitioners to adopt more participatory and collaborative ways. As Hess (2013) points out, there are shifts underway in how learning happens in the 21st century. Christian educators, working in a globalized world, need to be attentive to these shifts in order to design learning experiences that are effective and constructive for today's learners.

71

Conclusion

This paper has considered how Christian adult learning is interrupted by emerging practices in online pedagogy and asked how this might be understood and interpreted by theological educators. The online community of inquiry has been presented as a pedagogical approach, with an emphasis on cognitive, social, and teaching presence for quality and effective online learning. Reference has been made to research literature and personal online practitioner experience. Particular attention has been given to Boeve's theology of interruption. Insights have been drawn from his concept of theological interruption to propose that online pedagogy is interruptive in its capacity to influence and shape the online environment for adult theological learning. This invites further discussion about future theological education in new virtual spaces.

Notes

1. Core-component courses are Old Testament, New Testament, Christology, Church, Sacraments, and Moral Theology. The remaining components are specialist electives chosen from areas of practical theology such as Philosophy of Christian Education; Mission, Ethos, and Values in the Church School; Catholic Social Teaching; Chaplaincy; Engaging with World Religions; Liturgy and Collective Worship; Youth Ministry; and Parish Catechesis. The specialist components are determined by each local provider.

References

Ascough, R. (2007). Welcoming design: Hosting a hospitable online course. *Teaching Theology and Religion, 10*(3), 131–136.

Astley, J. (2002). *Ordinary theology: Looking, listening and learning in theology.* Farnham, Surrey: Ashgate.

Boeve, L. (2007). *God interrupts history: Theology in a time of upheaval.* New York: Continuum.

Boeve, L. (2009a). The shortest definition of religion: Interruption 1. *The Pastoral Review, 5*(3), 4–9.

Boeve, L. (2009b). The shortest definition of religion: Interruption 2. *The Pastoral Review, 5*(4), 4–9.

Boeve, L. (2009c). The shortest definition of religion: Interruption 3. *The Pastoral Review,* 5(5), 18–25.

Brennan, R. (2003). One size doesn't fit all: Pedagogy in the online environment. Volume 1. *National Centre for Vocational Education Research.* Retrieved from http://www.ncver.edu.au/10707/58201

Brookfield, S. (1986). *Understanding and facilitating adult learning.* Milton Keynes: Open University Press.

Bruner, J. (1986). *Actual minds, possible worlds.* Cambridge, MA: Harvard University Press.

Buber, M. (2002). *Between man and man.* London: Routledge.

Campbell, H. (2005). *Exploring religious community online.* New York: Peter Lang Publishing.

Carusi, A. (2003). Taking philosophical dialogue online. *Discourse: Learning and Teaching in Philosophical and Religious Studies,* 3(1), 95–156.

De Bary, E. (2003). *Theological reflection: The creation of spiritual power in the information age.* Collegeville, MN: Liturgical Press.

Dewey, J. (1966). *John Dewey: Selected educational writings* (F. Garforth, Ed.). London: Heinemann Educational Books.

Dinges, W. (2006). Faith, hope and (excessive) individualism. In R. Imbelli (Ed.), *Handing on the faith: The church's mission and challenge* (pp. 30–43). New York: Crossroad.

D'Orsa, T. (2013). Catholic curriculum: Re-framing the conversation. *International Studies in Catholic Education,* 5(1), 68–82.

Downes, S. (2007). Learning networks in practice. *BECTA Emerging Technologies for Learning.* Retrieved from http://www.becta.org.uk/research

Freire, P. (1972). *Pedagogy of the oppressed.* Harmondsworth: Penguin.

Garrison, D., Anderson, T., & Archer, W. (2000). Critical inquiry in a text-based environment: Computer conferencing in higher education. *The Internet and Higher Education,* 2(2–3), 87–105.

Gresham, J. (2006). The divine pedagogy as a model for online education. *Teaching Theology and Religion,* 9(1), 24–28.

Gulati, S. (2004). *Constructivism and emerging online pedagogy: a discussion for formal to acknowledge and promote the informal.* Annual Conference of Universities Association for Continuing Education. Retrieved from http://www.leeds.ac.uk/educol/documents/00003562.htm

Hess, M. (2005). *Engaging technology in theological education. All that we can't leave behind.* Lanham, MD, and Oxford: Rowman & Littlefield.

Hess, M. (2013). A new culture of learning: Implications of digital culture for communities of faith. *Communication Research Trends,* 32(3), 13–20.

Holmes, B., & Gardner, J. (2006). *E-learning concepts and practice.* London: SAGE.

Huang, H. (2002). Toward constructivism for adult learners in online learning environments. *British Journal of Educational Technology, 33*(1), 27–37.

Knowles, M. (1980). *The modern practice of adult education: From pedagogy to andragogy*. Wilton, CT: Association Press.

Kop, R. (2007). Blogs and wikis as disruptive technologies; Is it time for a new pedagogy? In M. Osborne, M. Houston, & N. Toman (Eds.), *The Pedagogy of Lifelong Learning* (pp. 192–202). London and New York: Routledge.

Lee, K. (2010). *Faith-based education that constructs*. Eugene, OR: Wipf & Stock.

Lewis, R. (2007). A Review of: "Engaging technology in theological education: All that we can't leave behind." *Religious Education, 102*(4), 455–460.

Mason, R., & Rennie, F. (2008). *E-learning and social networking handbook*. London and New York: Routledge

Mezirow, J. (1991). *Transformative dimensions of adult learning*. San Francisco: Jossey-Bass.

Meyer, K. (2010). The role of disruptive technology in the future of higher education. *Educause Quarterly Magazine, 33*(1). Retrieved from http://www.educause.edu/ero/article/role-disruptive-technology-future-higher-education.

Morgan-Klein, B., & Osborne, M. (2007). *The concepts and practices of lifelong learning*. London and New York: Routledge.

Palmer, P. (1998). *The courage to teach: Exploring the inner landscape of a teacher's life*. San Francisco: Jossey-Bass.

Palloff, R., & Pratt, K. (2007). *Building learning communities in cyberspace: Effective strategies for the virtual classroom*. (2nd. ed.). San Francisco: Jossey-Bass.

Regan, J. (2002). *Toward an adult church*. Chicago: Loyola Press.

Rossiter, G. (1999). Historical perspective on the development of catholic religious education in Australia: Some implications for the future. *Journal of Religious Education, 47*(1), 5–18.

Sajjadi, S. (2008). Religious education and information technology: Challenges and problems. *Teaching Theology and Religion, 11*(4), 185–190.

Salmon, G. (2003). *E-moderating: The key to teaching and learning online*, London, Kogan Page.

Schön, D. (1983). *The reflective practitioner: How professionals think in action*. New York: Basic Books.

Siemens, G. (2004). *Connectivism: A learning theory for the digital age*. Retrieved from http://www.elearnspace.org/Articles/connectivism.html

Stephenson, J. (2001). *Teaching and learning online: Pedagogies for new technologies*. London, Kogan Page.

Stern, J. (2013). *Progression in learning: Research by pupils, teachers and advisors*. Paper presented at AREIAC Conference 2013, Liverpool.

Stone, H., & Durk, J. (2006). *How to think theologically.* Philadelphia: Fortress Press.

Stuart-Buttle, R. (2011). Communicating faith and online learning. In J. Sullivan (Ed.), *Communicating Faith* (pp. 328–343). Washington, DC: The Catholic University of America Press.

Stuart-Buttle, R. (2013). Virtual theology, faith and adult education. Newcastle upon Tyne: Cambridge Scholars Publishing.

Swan, K., Shea, P., Richardson, J., Ice, P., Garrison, D., Cleveland-Innes, M., & Arbaugh, J. (2008). Validating a measurement tool of presence in online communities of inquiry. *E-Mentor, 2*(24), 1–12.

Vygotsky, L. (1962). *Thought and language.* Cambridge, MA: MIT Press.

Weller, M. (2007). *Virtual learning environments. Using, choosing and developing your VLE.* London and New York: Routledge.

Zukowski, A. (2000). Kaizening into the future: Distance education. In T. Hunt, T. Oldenski, & T. Wallace (Eds.), *Catholic School Leadership* (pp. 174–188). London and New York: Falmer Press.

JECB 18:1 (2014): 77–132   1366-5456

Book Reviews

JECB 18:1 (2014): 80–82   1366-5456

Elisabeth Arweck and Robert Jackson (eds.)
Religion, Education, and Society
New York: Routledge, 2014 hb 171pp $145.00
ISBN 978-0-415-82472-9

Religion, Education, and Society collects current research findings focusing on young people and their relationship to religion in their education. This research presents insights on how Religious Education (RE) is taught in secondary schools in the United Kingdom. Chapters of particular interest were 5, 8, and 11.

In chapter 5, James C. Conroy, David Lundie, and Vivienne Baumfield provide background on religious education as an element of the search for meaning. Due to this shift in thinking, students are making their own meaning through RE, as opposed to attending to the truth claims of a religion. This chapter attempted to investigate how questions of meaning are treated daily in classrooms. Case studies presented offered insights into student perceptions of religious education and this meaning-making process. The authors found that with multiple paths to meaning, RE fails to create any kind of ethical meaning for students. Conroy, Lundie, and Baumfield conclude that the claims of religious community must first be affirmed before meaning can be constructed through shared experiences of culture, religion, and events.

In chapter 8, Judith Everington presents a research study focused on a cohort of English trainee teachers of religious education and the role their personal life knowledge played in their teaching and understanding of teacher-student relationships. The cohort of fourteen beginning teachers included a mix of Muslims, Christians, atheists, agnostics or undecided, and one Sikh. Through regular discussions and questionnaires, data were gathered to determine the extent to which personal life knowledge was used in the cohort's teaching. Although they used their personal knowledge in varying ways and for different purposes, all the teachers believed personal knowledge was valuable in the teaching of religious education. Everington also discusses some of the dangers and benefits of this openness. Her findings suggest a need for teacher trainees to have opportunities to reflect on the practice of sharing their personal life knowledge with students. Everington made a good case for sharing personal life knowledge in the teaching of RE.

The essay in chapter 9 focuses on the contribution of Swedish teach-ers to the integration of Swedish Muslims. Jenny Berglund focuses on the question, who do you talk to when you are concerned or worried about something? Respondents were allowed to choose five of fourteen options that included "parent," "teacher," and "priest," to name a few. Among her findings Berglund discovered that compared to 5% of the rest of the respondents, 50% of those identifying themselves as Muslim indicated they confided in teachers for help. Berglund discussed possible reasons for this finding. These included Swedish teachers' ability to establish and maintain relationships of trust with students. She also explored cultural aspects of Islam in relation to contemporary Swedish culture. The essay begins an interesting dialogue on the benefits of relationships between Muslim students and their teachers that can be continued by the reader. Berglund concludes with suggestions for further research on the relational dimensions of teaching as well as Muslim-specific teacher training. This research could improve the ability of teachers in European countries to have a positive influence on Muslim students.

Chapters 1, 2, and 11 also have stimulating insights regarding RE. In chapter 1, Julia Ipgrave focuses on relationships between local religious practices and the attitudes of young people to those of their peers. Her findings are surprising, inasmuch as RE had less impact on young people than the religion in the neighborhood and being "religious." Olga Schi-halejev's essay in chapter 2 reviews a quantitative project related to young people's attitudes toward religious diversity. Chapter 11 is a particularly interesting essay focusing on the purposes of Christian youth work. In this essay Naomi Stanton explores how such youth work serves to build com-munities of faith that will continue as youth become adults. Key findings include relationships and engagement as ways to connect young people to churches as they become young adults.

The rest of the chapters focus on varying topics related to current issues in RE. These include young people's attitudes toward religion, per-spectives on the psychology of religion, and reflections on religion from young British Sikhs. This collection of essays and research studies provides much background and information on RE; yet with any edited volume, the voice of the authors vary, as do the research designs. Taken as a whole, the collection gathered by the editors provides a thought-provoking variety of information that moves the reader to think more deeply about RE.

This book would serve as a great resource for anyone researching RE or working in the field of RE who desires more background on the current challenges and research in RE.

Randall J. King

JECB 18:1 (2014): 82–84   1366-5456

Jeff Astley, Leslie J. Francis, Mandy Robbins, and Mualla Selçuk (eds.)
Teaching Religion, Teaching Truth:
Theoretical and Empirical Perspectives
Bern: Peter Lang, 2012 pb 281pp $53.95
ISBN 978- 3-0343-0818-3

Can religious educators respond to the opportunities and challenges of religious plurality without ignoring, or seeking to resolve, competing truth claims? After reading the essays in *Teaching Religion, Teaching Truth: Theoretical and Empirical Perspectives*, I felt as if I had taken an exceptional course in wisdom. The editors selected erudite Christian and Islamic scholars to speak from within their own traditions, inviting us to listen deeply, openly, critically, and respectfully—in short, inviting us to learn. At fourteen essays ranging from theoretical to empirical, the breadth and depth are considerable. Readers will be enriched by the thought-provoking insights of these Turkish, Western European, American, Canadian, and Australian scholars.

The book is divided into four parts. Part 1 offers five essays from Roman Catholic and Protestant perspectives. Part 2 contains three essays written from Muslim perspectives. Part 3 brings empiricism to bear, with four studies focusing on the faith development of children growing up within religious plurality. The final section, written by one of the editors, Jeff Astley, is entitled *A Theological Reflection on the Nature of Religious Truth*. It asks provocative questions about dialogic pedagogy and the nature of truth itself.

Part 1 begins with the reminder of Vatican II's declaration on theology of religions, asserting that all religions can be "ways of salvation" and that "God is speaking other languages besides Christian" (Durka, p. 17). Next, D'Souza clarifies the terms *plurality* and *pluralism*: "plurality" is defined as multiplicity, and "pluralism" is defined as a positive attitude about plurality. Schweitzer expands the concept of pluralism with his integration of *principled pluralism*, based on the principles of dialogue, tolerance, and mutual respect, saying that "dialogue is not the end of difference, and differences should not be the end of dialogue" (p. 39). D'Souza agrees, suggesting that religious educators mistakenly either attempt to focus solely on common religious and moral principles, ignoring otherwise edifying differences, or seek to banish religiosity from the conversation altogether. D'Souza insists that we need both our commonality and our distinctiveness (p. 59).

Cascante-Comez writes from the context of the pluralist theology of liberation, grounded in the actions of testimony, dialogue, and service. Testimony requires public acts and behaviors grounded in the values of love and justice. Dialogue requires religious educators to provide opportunities for students to expand their capacity for hospitality to the religious "other" (p. 74). Service requires "'faith that expresses itself through love' in the world . . . for the sake of justice and peace of the world" (p. 75).

Part 2 is written by Islamic scholars. Selçuk provides an instructive examination of Islamic pedagogy, with an in-depth exploration of the term *hikmah* (wisdom) revealing Islam to be "a religion of conscience based on individualistic choice and responsibility" (p. 104). Next, Doğan explores a pluralistic understanding of Islam, rooted in the Constitution of Madina. Doğan calls for religious educators to "create a culture of compromise, tolerance, and trustworthiness" (p. 117). Finally, Arslan suggests that religious educators should teach from the perspective of *fitrah* (the wholeness of the human being) thus promoting students' capacities to see one another, and themselves, multidimensionally.

In part 3, plurality is explored empirically and pedagogically. Arweck and Nesbitt examine the experiences of young people raised in mixed-faith families. Suggested as a microcosm of processes that occur for all people living among a plurality of religions, the study reported evidence of the capacity for humans to navigate cultural and religious differences with respect, as they hold space for each other's "otherness." Ziebertz compares attitudes about religious differences of young people, ages sixteen through seventeen years old, living across ten countries, alerting religious educators to the need to help students deepen their religious identities without "hardening into fundamentalism or, at the other extreme, losing their profile entirely through modifying their own convictions" (p. 181). Francis and Robbins examine data that suggest a person's tendency toward exclusivity or inclusivity correlates with sensing versus intuitive personality types, respectively. The final essay is a theological critique in which Astley contends that while dialogic pedagogy is crucial, the important dialogue is not between the religions, but between the individual and his or her world.

Teaching Religion, Teaching Truth: Theoretical and Empirical Perspectives is a compelling and important read. I recommend it to all religious educators dedicated to promoting salvific dialogue. The reality of our plurality is undeniable. With hospitality and humility, we can learn to listen deeply and speak well. These dedicated religious educators show us how to learn and, by learning, how to teach.

Eileen Mejia

JECB 18:1 (2014): 84–86   1366-5456

Sylvia Baker
Swimming against the Tide:
The New Independent Christian Schools and Their Teenage Pupils
Oxford: Peter Lang, 2013 pb 249pp £42.00
ISBN 978-3-0343-0942-4

This book deals with the emergence of the new Christian schools in Britain which were founded from the 1960s onwards. The opening chapters outline the social and theological background to the formation of the schools in the UK which, in the main, came either from Reformed roots or as result of the more radical side of the charismatic movement. As a result of their common suspicion of the secularization of the state system of education, the new Christian schools, despite their separate origins, came to be similar in many ways. They collaborated to the extent of forming a common trust (CST) which gave them all an umbrella, and they also noted their affinities with Jewish and Islamic schools, which had a similar suspicion of the state sector. The new Christian schools, which are open to OFSTED inspection, have a specific understanding of the need for a Christian curriculum which, in their view, should contain a strong bias against the teaching of biological evolution as an indisputable scientific truth. Even so, the new Christian schools came to be influenced by the

National Curriculum since few of them educated pupils right up to the age of 18. They needed to prepare their pupils to transfer into the state system at some point before this. Chapter 4 gives an interesting and well-informed account of the sometimes acrimonious political debate engendered by the new Christian schools and the various politicized arguments relating to their existence, as these were mediated through changes in employment law and by court judgments. The chapter is sufficiently well informed to correct Geoffrey Walford, long-time critic of the new Christian schools, at several points.

The book is designed to ascertain whether the purpose for which the schools were founded and the criticisms of them made by their opponents are supported by empirical evidence. Prior to the doctoral project on which this book is based, there were no substantial data on which any judgement of this kind could be made, and, as result, this book offers a valuable set of insights both to policy-makers in the upper echelons of government and to more informed commentators on educational issues. Baker collected data from 695 teenage pupils receiving their education in 22 of the new Christian schools, and she presents an analysis of a multiplicity of findings by reference to the themes relevant to the debate on the origin and purpose of the Christian schools which has been described earlier. In other words, the empirical data are specifically suited to answering the contentious questions which have been raised by friends and critics of the schools. In addition, the data, where appropriate, are compared with Leslie Francis's large-scale study of maintained schools so as to contrast the beliefs and values of pupils at the new Christian schools with those of similar age in mainstream education. In this way, it is possible to see to what extent the pupils of the new Christian schools differ from the majority of their age group in terms of morality, well-being, religious beliefs, on opinions on creation-evolution, drug-taking and substance abuse, and a host of other issues. Baker analyzes her data using chi-square significance tests, and she comments on each block of items relating to a particular theme. By way of further analysis a series of comparisons are made between sub-groups: between males and females, older and younger pupils, and those peoples within the new Christian schools who are not affiliated with Christianity themselves and others who are.

The text concludes with well-balanced chapters selecting the most salient findings and placing them in the context of the discussion in the pre-empirical chapters. The findings indicate that pupils attending the new Christian schools give every indication of being good citizens who have a perfectly reasonable attitude to science. That is, the pupils are willing to accept empirical evidence for theoretical assertions and to work in such a way that they would be able to obtain jobs within the scientific and technical sectors of the public economy. The point here is that the pupils from these schools are not sectarian, but could enter mainstream debate or employment. Until now, some have thought that pupils at the new Christian schools were in danger of being marginalized once their education was complete.

The book is succinctly written, has an extensive bibliography, and contains an appendix on methodology. Baker carried out her research according to current ethical protocols. I thoroughly recommend *Swimming against the Tide*.

William Kay

JECB 18:1 (2014): 86–88   1366-5456

Dietrich Bonhoeffer
Theological Education at Finkenwalde: 1935–1937. Dietrich Bonhoeffer Works, Volume 14 (Translated by Douglas W. Stott; edited by H. Gaylon Barker and Mark S. Brocker)
Minneapolis: Augsburg/Fortress Press, 2013 pb 1014pp $75.00
ISBN 978-1-4514-2587-1

Dietrich Bonhoeffer had been pastor to two German congregations in London, England, in the early 1930s but felt compelled to identify with the church in Germany that was protesting the rulings of the Third Reich. He agreed to return to Germany to oversee the theological formation of candidates for ministry in the Confessing Church at the Finkenwalde Preachers' Seminary that met in what is now part of Szczecin City, Poland. The 14th volume in the massive Bonhoeffer Works project brings together letters, lecture notes, sermon manuscripts, and related documents from this period.

There are three dominant themes that emerge in the letters, the lectures, and the sermons. First, there is the obvious political climate—the extraordinary tension under which they pursued their common life together and their studies, made more poignant for the reader who already knows that the Gestapo would close the seminary in the early fall of 1937.

The second dominant theme is ecclesiology—again, understandable in that Finkenwalde represented a protest against the official and government-endorsed church that, for Bonhoeffer and his colleagues, had lost its right to be called the church. Bonhoeffer's theology of the church comes through in the letters, but especially in the lectures, including a defining essay given on a retreat, entitled "Church Communion." Bonhoeffer stands within the Reformed tradition when he speaks of the way in which Word and sacrament demarcate the life of the church; but he further stresses that the true church is animated by Spirit and lives in radical obedience to Christ and that thus, Christ and Christ alone has final authority over the church (not, in other words, the German government). A related theme, ecumenism, emerges regularly—particularly when it comes to the relationship of the Confessing Church to other communions, notably in Sweden and England.

Finally, the third dominant theme is the formal curriculum and community practices of Finkenwalde. While liturgical leadership and other aspects of pastoral ministry were taught, this was clearly first and foremost a "preachers" seminary, with a high emphasis on the exposition of the Scriptures. Thus exegesis and Bible study, along with the practice of biblical exposition, dominated the curriculum. Theology and practice of preaching are a significant focus—indeed, the lecture on the preaching office and the work of homiletics is Bonhoeffer at his best, particularly as he nuances the relationship between preaching and the Scriptures and between the Scriptures and Christ.

Also noteworthy is that the lectures were given within an intentional or ordered community. For those familiar with Bonhoeffer's *Life Together*, it was in Finkenwalde where the daily routine of prayer and confession— "a day together"—was lived out. One of the most fascinating exchanges in this collection is Bonhoeffer's correspondence with Karl Barth on this theme. Bonhoeffer writes to the senior theologian: "Theological work and genuine pastoral community emerges only from within a life defined by morning and evening reflection on the word and by fixed times of prayer . . ." (p. 254). Barth's response, interestingly enough, is not too enthusiastic, when he speaks of being "bothered . . . by the smell . . . of monastic eros and pathos . . . for which I for now have . . . [no] real use . . ."! Bonhoeffer was clearly undeterred; he continued to insist that theological study needed both critical theological reflection as well as the practice of meditation and daily common prayer. Indeed, the essay on meditation that comes later in the collection is as fine as one will find anywhere by anyone on this topic. Bonhoeffer viewed this broader curriculum as essential to the sanctification of his emerging preachers—and, indeed, the call to discipleship and sanctification, as the essential complement to the experience of justification is the theological basis for this call to an intentional community.

The collection includes an extensive and invaluable introduction by the English editor, an afterword by the German editor, and a very helpful set of appendixes and indexes. If there is anything of questionable value in the collection, it might be the lecture notes by Bonhoeffer's students—presumably in lieu of Bonhoeffer's actual lecture notes. These may have archival value, but they represent at best student impressions and insights—all good, but not necessarily what Bonhoeffer himself intended in his lectures (as all university and seminary professors surely know). But, all in all, an invaluable publication, and an indispensable contribution to the history of theological education.

Gordon T. Smith

JECB 18:1 (2014): 88–90   1366-5456

Oddrun M. H. Bråten
Towards a Methodology for Comparative Studies in Religious Education: A Study of England and Norway
Münster: Waxmann, 2013 pb 233pp €32.90
ISBN 978-3-8309-2887-4

The growing demand for interculturality and multi-religiosity in national educational systems is challenging the traditional approach to Religious Education. From an international perspective, a systematic comparative approach to RE in different countries seems necessary to identify and reflect the current needs for RE in national educational contexts.

In her PhD thesis, Bråten aspired to respond to this challenge. Her first intention was to examine and compare the *national imaginaries* of two countries "in relation to the choice of attempting a multi-faith approach to RE in their state schools" (p. 207). Being a Norwegian, Bråten decided to compare Norway with England because she was interested in understanding the context of English RE. Her effort to develop a systematic approach to comparative methodology "led her to a place that she could not have foreseen or even imagined when she started her research" (p. 209). It "grew to be a key element" (p. 208) of her study. The result of her effort is a specific combination of comparative approaches which she calls "a general model for comparative studies in RE" (p. 194).

It is interesting to follow the way of how Bråten unfolds her methodology. Based on previous research and theoretical approaches to RE described in chapter 1, Bråten decided to use two sets of ideas to lead her through her investigation. First, she applied the idea of three dimensions necessary for her comparison: supranational, national, and subnational processes. Formal supranational processes refer to international educational policy; informal ones to secularization, pluralization, and globalization. These dimensions penetrate all chapters of her book.

The second set, characterized in chapters 2, 5, and 8, was formed by the idea of four levels of RE curriculum. They were used to structure her thesis: the societal level described in chapter 3, the institutional level in chapter 4, the instructional level in chapter 6, and the experiential level in chapter 7. On the societal level Bråten focused specifically on the role of academic disciplines in the development of multi-faith approaches to RE and on the analysis of the main two 'power texts' in academic debates. On the institutional level she compared relevant legal texts and curricula. To compare the instructional and experiential level, she explored RE teachers' and students' opinions on several RE topics. In chapter 5, Bråten tries to tie the use of field data to the overall methodology, using concepts such as *civil enculturation* and *national imaginaries*.

The combination of both approaches allowed Bråten to avoid some 'dry' linear or traditionally hierarchical relations between the levels and led to the creation of a genuine diagrammatical model of the methodology of RE comparative research. I also appreciate Bråten's self-reflection in writing openly about her obstacles and limitations, as well as her suggestions of the future development of her methodology in comparing 'different national styles' and 'inclusive RE and construction of otherness' (p. 209).

In my view, the results of Bråten's thesis have the potential to enrich her readers not only by its collection of interesting data but also by the beauty of her logical thinking. This is not only my impression, for she won the award for Outstanding Research Student of 2009–2010 at the University of Warwick, England. Even her own understanding of Norwegian context was increased as a direct result of application of this methodology (p. 208).

On the other hand, the fact that this book was written as a PhD thesis also manifests symptoms of this genre. The author had to explain all procedures, including minor exceptions, in considerable detail.

What I miss in Bråten's work is more mention of the influence of family upbringing upon construction of RE knowledge and attitudes of children and youth. It could have been an important factor, changing the dynamics of relationships between elements on instructional and experiential level. I would also add some basic statistical data about development of a population's religiosity in both countries (e.g. according to census).

Despite those comments, I truly believe Bråten's methodological model might be considered a template for comparative studies in RE. It is transferable to other regions, such as to the Central European context where I work as an RE researcher. Reading this book gave me a clear idea of holistic approach to research in RE, and that is why I recommend it to others planning to carry out research in RE.

Dana Hanesová

JECB 18:1 (2014): 90–92   1366-5456

Christian J. Churchill and Gerald E. Levy
The Enigmatic Academy: Class, Bureaucracy, and Religion in American Education
Philadelphia: Temple University Press, 2012 pb 223pp $27.86
ISBN 978-1-4399-0784-9

The Enigmatic Academy is an account of 40 years of collaborative social research into the role education plays in American culture and class. The cooperation between Churchill and Levy gives this book its depth and lends interest to the case studies described within. As the authors share their findings and some possible implications of their research at three American educational institutions that serve different social classes, they both succeed and fall short at different points in the book.

From the outset, Churchill and Levy are open and honest with readers regarding their theoretical persuasion. They write, "We confirm Karl Marx's assumption that education, as an instrument of social control, supports the concentration of wealth and power in the upper classes while coordinating the middle and lower classes in the service of that concentration" (p. 2). In the book's introduction, the authors provide a clear and thorough framework for the reader to understand the scope and focus of their research. The succinctness of the introduction stands in contrast with the verbosity of the chapters that follow, and this difference creates the feeling that this is a 12-page book with 200+ pages of appendixes and field notes to wade through.

This social-control view of education consistently influences their account of each institution they study, and particularly that of the Landover Job Corps Center. That said, they give much space in the following chapters trying to account for the tension between Marx's stance and the view many hold of public education as a leveling agent and factor in increased social mobility among classes. The authors use the expression "secular redemption" (p. 2) to describe this belief in education as a means for people to better themselves and improve their quality of life. Beyond this reference to education's redemptive possibilities, they give little space to the role of religion or spirituality in educational institutions. Most of *The Enigmatic Academy* is devoted to analyzing the role of class in terms of how schools and colleges serve the specific populations involved in the three institutions studied.

Churchill and Levy succeed with their full disclosure as to the level of personal involvement they have had in each of the institutions studied. This is particularly important because they have chosen a private liberal arts college at which they were both personally involved as both student and instructor, a private preparatory school for wayward boys from upper class families where one researcher worked during this study, and a job corps center with which neither of them was personally involved. The difference in their personal involvement among the three schools is reflected in the fluctuating objectivity of their observations. For example, most of the observations related to the liberal arts college and the preparatory school were descriptive of students and staff, while their reflections related to the job corps center were more definitive, as reflected in their assertion, "Perhaps the most poignant illusion in American education is the promise that the lower classes need only be educated to realize the American dream" (p. 123). Such claims are few and far between, but they illustrate the ebb and flow of the authors' attempt to maintain their role as observers while also being able to interject sociological insights that account for the tension in these schools between staff, students, and administration.

Like walking through dense underbrush, this book leads the reader on a long and meandering journey that is not focused around a coherent theme but rather takes its cues from the researchers' accounts of their observations. Readers waiting for the authors to present a unifying theory other than their beginning theoretical beliefs will be kept waiting to the end. Rather, the authors use *The Enigmatic Academy* to illustrate how these three institutions interact with dynamics of social class, power, stakeholders, and institutional change. As each school evolves through changing leadership, staff, clientele, and social and political contexts, the most notable and captivating interactions occur between the administration, instructors, and students. Churchill and Levy succeed in their thorough description of these groups in terms of their respective hopes, motivations, and ability to create change on an organizational level.

The Enigmatic Academy would serve well as a course text related to qualitative research, or perhaps as a book study for a group well-read in sociology. For others wanting to take on a research project of this considerable scope and length, this book may also serve as a worthwhile roadmap. The complex interactions that power, control, and social change have on educational institutions is a reality that deserves more understanding and Churchill and Levy's research provides a considerable contribution toward this growing body of insight.

Chris Cochran

JECB 18:1 (2014): 92–95   1366-5456

James C. Conroy et al.
Does Religious Education Work? A Multi-dimensional Investigation
London: Bloomsbury Academic, 2013 pb 208pp £75.00
ISBN 978-1-4411-2799-0

This publication represents the findings of a major "Religion and Society" research project initiated in 2007 by the UK Arts and Humanities Research

Council and the Economic and Social Research Council. The three-year project was led by scholars from the University of Glasgow, King's College London, and Queen's University Belfast.

The size and scope of the project are impressive. The research was driven at the professorial level, drawing on expertise in theology, anthropology, and psychology, as well as education, and involved teams of fieldworkers investigating twenty-four different schools across England, Scotland, and Northern Ireland. The omission of Wales is justified because RE was seen to be structured and delivered under the same system as England 'at the time the research was first conceived' (p. 16). The recognition that it has diverged in the years since then merely underlines further the diversity in Religious Education across the United Kingdom. The authors, quite justifiably I believe, argue that RE differs across the constituent nations even more than do other curriculum subjects.

Those in countries where Religious Education is absent from the public education system are probably already bemused by its obligatory nature in the UK. To discover that policies and practice vary across the nations of the UK can only add to their bemusement, but one of the strengths of this book is the way it makes one consider the different approaches that are possible for a compulsory RE programme, albeit approaches that have changed over recent decades.

'A somewhat odd volume' is how Conroy and his colleagues describe their book (p. 1), which is one of the fruits of the research project. The investigation they have conducted is avowedly multi-dimensional. They admit that their methodology leads to findings from which it is hard to generalize, but they are more concerned with getting under the skin of the subject, uncovering its 'inscape' (to borrow a term from the poet Hopkins) and posing provoking questions. This is not a work that follows the path of some lazy post-modern approaches, hiding behind the irony found in discontinuities. There is a genuine attempt to address the question in the title: *Does* Religious Education work? And what do we want it to do anyway? Any educational research, they argue, will inevitably be normative as well as descriptive and analytical, because 'education is ineluctably a normative activity' (p. 2). Their research is not just an attempt to understand how Religious Education functions, but also 'to contribute to capacity-building in the study of RE' (p. 3).

The book is in two parts. Part 1 deals with methodological and structural questions, and part 2 with the substance of Religious Education. The authors begin by looking at *why* Religious Education is such a strange subject. Differences in legislation across the UK mean that although education in general looks very different across the constituent nations, the desired outcomes are remarkably similar. Except in RE—here, 'the imperatives differ somewhat across the United Kingdom and between schools serving different communities' (p. 4).

Much previous research into Religious Education in the UK either has adopted a philosophical and normative approach or has employed quantitative analysis of students' attitudes and dispositions. This project, however, is located mainly in qualitative research: reflections on policy lead to a largely ethnographic approach, with an eclectic bundle of add-ons: Delphi methods, Actor Network Theory, student questionnaires, and analysis of texts. Chapter 1 gives an overview of the methodology, which itself reflects the strangeness of the subject, explored further in chapter 2, which is aptly entitled 'The Strange Position of Education in Religion in Contemporary Political Culture'. The complexities of UK policy and practice are analysed in chapter 3, before a discussion of the confusions and challenges posed by three particular conceptual questions in chapter 4: the rationale for RE, the role of the teacher (their principles and pedagogy), and the significance of truth claims in RE.

The substance of the research emerges in part 2, although this is by no means a blow-by-blow account of what the ethnography uncovered. The schedules and questionnaires are published in detail in the appendices; the main text, however, concentrates on key emergent themes. One senses that the range of schools in the survey reflects stronger divergences in practice than do policy differences between the systems in England, Scotland, and Northern Ireland. Denominational schools, particularly Roman Catholic schools, are distinctive in more ways than one. All the schools in the survey (which are given pseudonyms) are within the public education system. Their varying levels of participation reflect to some extent their commitment to the delivery of RE. This emerges in the discussions. Chapter 5 explores the extent to which RE contributes to the inculcation of good citizenship and 'committed pluralism'—what is the place of the 'other' in RE's social and civic aims? Chapter 6 considers the importance of the textbooks used in RE—an emergent theme that seems to have surprised the researchers. To what extent is pedagogy controlled less by the teacher and more by text books published to prepare students for examinations at the age of 16? This feature, it is acknowledged, may have arisen because the research was focused mainly on students in Year 10 or its equivalent. Chapters 7 and 8 deal with two other aspects arising from the study—the stories communities of practice tell themselves about RE and student perspectives on the subject. Data for the latter were derived from question-naires, the most quantitative part of the research, though not necessarily the most reliable, as the level of response was skewed towards schools (notably Catholic) where RE is held in higher regard. However, that result in itself contributes to the overall story.

A concluding chapter, 'Imagining and Re-Imagining Religious Educa-tion', reverts to the more philosophical and reflective. It includes a rather ironic note: many students enjoy RE, it appears, but not always for the right reasons. 'If the goal of RE was to relax and have a good laugh, then we might observe that it did indeed work', say the authors (p. 226). But Conroy et al. conclude with a question of some profundity: 'Should classes in RE be enjoyable at the expense of the creation of a flat-pack theology, where students are somehow invited to build their own version of religion that embraces their spirituality but pays little attention to the linguistic and conceptual demands of the genealogically rich traditions of religious systems, and the otherness that they embody?' (p. 226).

I found myself concurring with the expected answer. But I also found the book had made me reflect again on my own experience—the Reli-gious Education I was taught and later taught myself, which I went on to research and later to inspect in schools across England. What do I expect it to achieve? As I chair my county's SACRE (Standing Advisory Council on RE) next week, how can my colleagues and I discover if RE in our neck of the woods is working? I feel better equipped to deal with this question having read this book.

Andrew Marfleet

JECB 18:1 (2014): 96–98   1366-5456

Joseph L. DeVitis and Tianlong Yu (eds.)
Character and Moral Education: A Reader
New York: Peter Lang, 2011 419pp $52.50
ISBN 978-1-4331-1099-3

This book collects thirty-three contemporary essays that address the strengths and weaknesses of character education programs for the moral development of children in public schools. The editors lead readers on a fascinating journey into the complexities of character education programs in American public schools. The book's main thesis is that character education is multilayered in both theory and application and cannot be neatly packaged into the curriculum as other key learning areas can be.

In part 1, the authors present a largely negative analysis of character education curricula. Most are skeptical of the necessity of character education if it is based on erroneous statistics about the moral decline of American society. After the first section, the reader is left with a much stronger understanding of the vast challenges that character education courses face. Part 2 presents a wider framework for attention to how character education might be understood and more effectively integrated.

After reading part 1, readers may be left with gloomy sentiments about character instruction; if they hope to find a positive case presented for character instruction they will be disappointed. The authors largely agree that prepackaged character programs provide a narrow, artificial, and dark view of human nature that ignores the structural problems of society (Purpel, p. 50). The main weaknesses of character education outlined in part 1 include the avoidance of difference and conflict, the absence of justice, the silencing of minority voices, a lack of moral outrage, and the preservation of the status quo.

Part 2 offers a very different investigation of moral education in schools. The authors consider moral education from the perspectives of feminism, Deweyism, and critical pedagogy. In part 2, the authors criticize the present state of education as bureaucratic and self-serving, while presenting a more hopeful vision of moral education based on justice and building a democratic society where everyone has a role to play. Schools acting alone in the moral training of children are limited and artificial. Knowing right from wrong is easy; having it matter when no one is looking is more important (Covaleskie, p. 171). As Glass notes, "Evils of the day cannot be kept at the bay of the schoolhouse door" (p. 230).

In chapter 13, Alfie Kohn argues that the implicit goal of character education programs is to maintain school discipline with a "fix-the-kid" approach. On Kohn's account, it is like "the teacher holding a mirror up to the student and saying, 'This is who you are, now stop it'" (p. 134). Like Kohn, most of the authors make the same error of highlighting only the epistemological complexities with moral education, while ignoring the more foundational metaphysical aspects. Kohn takes a rhetorical jab at those who advocate moral education based on religious convictions. Children should decide for themselves "which traditions are worth preserving and why" (p. 134). Like most of the authors, Kohn largely ignores religious and Aboriginal traditions that do pass on to the next generation time-honored behaviors and values that are identity forming and community centered.

In chapter 19, Ronald Glass favors a critical pedagogical approach to moral education. He believes that critical pedagogy would entice more people to act against injustice. However, Glass then goes on to caricature those who offer religious explanations for moral actions as people who "always know the right thing to do only when a person achieves the primacy of the sacred to draw upon" (p. 233). He reasons that the "moral obscurities and unresolvable uncertainties of everyday life" (p. 237) and a lack of religious consensus concerning what is moral, or not, disqualify religion as a sufficient foundational framework (p. 233). In part 2, Thayer-Bacon defends a feminist perspective, stating that "feminists emphasize our plurality and differences" (p. 244). This is why a moral ontological analysis would give the reader a balanced analysis to consider.

This book is appropriate reading for a religious and secular audience at the lay, college, or university level and for anyone interested in ethics, citizenship studies, and moral education. Each reading does not require a prior background in moral theory, yet by the end of each reading one has gained a better perspective of particular moral theories and the contemporary trends in character education today.

What can we learn from this book? Educators must wrestle with the complexities of moral education. Rather than find this a daunting or misguided task, they should consider complexity in moral education a strength which can be drawn upon to include more effectively the theoretical and religious perspectives of other individuals and groups who are not always invited to participate in moral education policy and curricula.

The success of the book lies in its capacity to make transparent the current conversations in the moral education of children from many different perspectives. The readings will compel educators to question whether moral education should aim to reproduce the standards of present society or aim to transform society. New readers in particular will find this book to be beneficial for understanding the origins and perspectives of those political players who continue to discuss and debate school discipline, bullying, and violence in schools that continue to transpire in the media often on a weekly basis.

Matthew Etherington

JECB 18:1 (2014): 98–100   1366-5456

Ronald E. Heine
Origen: Scholarship in the Service of the Church
Oxford: Oxford University Press, 2010 pb 275pp $30.00
ISBN 978-0-19-920908-8

Ronald Heine has written a useful and scholarly work on the development of Origen's thought process. Heine discusses Origen's work within the context of two second-century locations. The book is divided into two parts. Each part commences with a discussion of the history, politics, and philosophical ideas present as Origen lives first in Alexandria and then is forced to move to Caesarea. During his formative period in Alexandria, the influence of the Gnostic community and its effects upon the Church occupied Origen's efforts. Heine describes some of the literature that the second-century writers produced in Alexandria, which would have a major impact upon Origen's thinking. Opportunity and provision to think and write came at the behest of Origen's patron, Ambrose, a former Valentinian Gnostic, who provided the means to work.

Heine portrays several second-century schools of believers and their teachers (pp. 48–64). These schools were not academic institutions as we know them today. Schools were led by men who served as spiritual guides to their students. Origen was a student of Clement and later a teacher himself. Greek philosophical thought was to train or form the character of the student, and this usually was accomplished through discussion and a study of various texts. The teacher and the student would study the texts to find the deeper hidden meanings, many of which were allegorically interpreted. Heine construes that Origen regarded himself as a Christian and was concerned about issues afflicting the local church in Alexandria.

In midlife, Origen moved to Caesarea, Palestine. His irreconcilable differences with Bishop Demetrius of Alexandria forced him to leave Alexandria. Origen's supporters in Palestine recognized his ability to interpret the Scriptures and provided him an opportunity to work. In order to deliver his homilies, he was ordained by the bishops of Caesarea and Jerusalem, which further angered Demetrius. It appears that the shift in his work was due to the sizable Jewish community and its relationship to Christianity. Through his friend Ambrose, Origen was able to work on issues such as prayer, martyrdom, and the Christian's relationship to the Law.

Heine describes that as Origen preached his homilies in Caesarea, hostility arose among the Jewish community. He argues that Origen needed to defend the use of the Law in the church and show how it was read and interpreted differently. As he studied the Old Testament, Origen had a strong focus on the Scriptures as they related to Jesus and the *Logos* of John 1. Heine points out that during this period of Origen's life, the hostility of the synagogue and the salvation of the Jews occupied much of Origen's attention. Yet even with these issues, Origen's ultimate goal was to build up the church. Heine illustrates, as Torjesen argues, "that the organizing center of Origen's homilies is the concept of the journey of the soul" (p. 184).

Origen produced a large amount of work from 238 to 244, a time of relative peace, including several commentaries and sermon collections. His work addressed the hardness of the Jews toward Christianity and showed the receptivity of the Gentiles as people of God. He used the Pauline texts to illustrate the hope of the Jews was their faith in Christ, as it was for the Gentile.

Heine closes the book with a chapter entitled "The Works and Themes of the Senior Scholar." In this chapter, he states that "in his *Commentary on Matthew* and *Against Celsus* Origen provides his most mature thinking" (p. 222). Origen's belief that some doctrines were exoteric (doctrine understood by the general population outside the church) and others esoteric (within the church) provides an excellent discussion of the growing depth of his thinking about the general population. Thus, doctrinal issues concerning the church became more important to Origen in his latter days.

These two geographical nexuses of Alexandria and Caesarea are significant because of the communal influences on Origen's theology. Origen is significant because he was the first systematic recorder of theology in defense of Christianity. The underpinning of the book is to contend that Origen's thinking was highly influenced by the two areas in which he lived and labored.

Heine's writing is clear, concise, and compact. His research is extensive and well presented. The book is a good read for the biblical scholar who would know more of the roots of Christianity or for an educational philosopher who would value a glimpse into the second-century thinking process.

Joseph Olson

JECB 18:1 (2014): 100–102   1366-5456

Thomas C. Hunt et al.
The Praeger Handbook of Faith-Based Schools
in the United States, K–12
Westport, CT: Greenwood, 2012 hb 2 vols 585pp $173.00
ISBN 978-0-313-39132-2

Faith-based schools have made a positive impact on many aspects of the religious and spiritual formation of students. Currently, 4.4 million children attend faith-based schools, and 1.5 million receive faith-based homeschooling in the USA. This two-volume reference surveys a variety of faith-based educational traditions in the United States, reviewing their respective rationales for faith-based schooling that receives no government support, and attempting to understand how those school traditions contribute to the common good.

The book provides historical overviews of each tradition, from the colonial period to the present. It includes information on supporting organizations and reviews significant issues for schools in those traditions. For example, some Amish and Mennonite schools emphasize manual labor and an agrarian lifestyle, rejecting modern technology. Some limit school-based learning to completion of the eighth grade. And whereas

Amish schools put more emphasis on the role of teachers, Mennonite schools are more student centered.

Calvinistic, Catholic, Lutheran, and Seventh-Day Adventist schools deeply connect the educational purpose with theological issues such as the sovereignty of God, the reality of sin, the centrality of salvation in Christ, and the renewal of this world. Calvinist schools view students as conservers, inquirers, and reformers. Catholic schools also view education as divine interventions to transform the world as God calls. Lutheran schools see education as the means by which societies live out their function of taming human selfishness and exchanging it for reason and social responsibility. Seventh-Day Adventist schools focus on the salvation of the student by restoring the image of God in humans. Probably the most innovative pedagogical approaches are introduced in Quaker schools, which exemplify inquiry-based learning, collaborative learning, experiential learning, learning through reflection, learning through service, and learning peace and social justice. Jewish, Greek Orthodox, and Islamic schools place the concerns of their religious community above those of the nation in which those respective communities forged their lives.

Based on the overall purpose of education, the *Praeger Handbook* divides faith-based schools into two categories. Amish, Mennonite, Lutheran, Quaker, and Seventh-Day Adventist schools focus on students' individual development, while Calvinist and Catholic schools seek to model and teach social responsibility so that students will be agents of the transformation of society.

The most critical question is probably whether faith-based schools are effective in producing positive learning outcomes. This book provides two kinds of evidence that faith-based schools accomplish this. First, students who have studied at faith-based schools outperform students in public schools in many academic areas. For example, students from faith-based schools have been shown to perform better on standardized tests than students from public schools, in each subject area and at each grade level tested. Second, faith-based schools also have a positive effect on aspects of the religious and spiritual formation of their students, helping create positive community values as well as individual moral behavior.

However, most faith-based schools have struggled with the same issues as public schools, such as the quality of education. Increased tuition fees to study at faith-based schools hinder many low-income families' children from attending. How can faith-based schools handle this issue? This book suggests that broad interreligious and ecumenical collaboration is needed among all participants in the private school sector, demonstrating perhaps that the contributors to this volume need to read more carefully their own words on why religious communities found independent schools in the first place.

This survey of faith-based schooling in the United States represents much hard work in gathering the wealth of information it presents. Libraries will be wise to purchase what should become an enduring reference.

HeeKap Lee

JECB 18:1 (2014): 102–4   1366-5456

Kevin E. Lawson (ed.)
Understanding Children's Spirituality
Eugene OR: Cascade Books, 2012 pb 438pp £39.00
ISBN 978-1-61097-525-4

This is an eclectic and engaging book, the third volume of papers from the Children's Spirituality Conference: Christian Perspectives, which is held triennially and focuses on equipping parents and churches in ministry with children. This book is from the 2009 conference and is in two parts. The first explores theological, historical, and social science research perspectives; and the second contexts of children's spirituality: family church and community. Authors range from renowned scholars to postgraduate students and practitioners. While it is clearly a book for academics and libraries, it is also useful for practitioners who want to understand some of the theological and theoretical underpinnings of their work and is written in an accessible manner to facilitate this.

The book starts off extremely strongly with chapters from eminent scholars Marcia Bunge on faith formation and William Brown on wisdom and play, but these are not just academic treatises; they are eminently practical offerings which can be translated into a local context. Bunge identifies six duties and responsibilities of parents and adults as well as six corresponding duties and responsibilities of children, along with eight best practices for nurturing the spiritual and moral lives of children. It would be fascinating to work out what an education programme for families based on this material would look like. Brown, a biblical scholar, offers an exegesis of some of the significant passages of Scripture on wisdom, but, importantly, he emphasizes the need to engage with wonder, to allow people to be rooted in and transformed by Scripture, and to create a world in which wisdom can play and be creative. He observes in conclusion that 'I can only imagine that as the disciples were deliberating among themselves about the import of their Lord's shocking pronouncement [about who is the greatest], Jesus and the child beside him, like God and Wisdom, were playing' (p. 37).

The remainder of the first section includes a chapter on the biblical metanarrative as seen by biblical storytellers, as well as several more historical chapters, including a Wesleyan perspective on sin and depravity, a chapter on the sacramental image of the child, based on the seventeenth-century priest Thomas Traherne, one on Irenaeus's stages of faith, one on baptismal practices, and chapters on spiritual development and spiritual formation. I particularly enjoyed Short's chapter, 'The Story That Grew', which shows how the biblical narrative has been interpreted and presented by biblical storytellers from Genesis to Acts, noting who the audience was, the location, and the turning point in the story (such as when Jacob blesses his sons and grandsons or Paul preaches the gospel to both Jews and Gentiles), the new element in the story, and the open question. She concludes that 'we tell children Bible stories to help them take their place in that great story, the true story about the world' (p. 57). Mosher's chapter on Irenaeus notes the lack of patristic writing in contemporary material on childhood and includes the comment that God never required understanding to begin to commune with God.

The second half includes twelve chapters which cover an encouraging breadth of contexts ranging among parents and families, church, sacraments, child protection, naming ceremonies, children's literature, foster care, and sickness. A particular highlight for me was Yust's chapter on intergenerational work, which contains practical suggestions related to facilitating intergenerational acts of worship whilst acknowledging that parents may struggle to know how to nurture their children. May, Stemp, and Burns discuss the place of children in new forms of church; I have seen little previous material on this. While there were quite mixed results from their research regarding the level of integration of children, perhaps the most interesting finding was that 'generational barriers seemed non-existent if the focal point of worship was the communion table' (p. 257). Csinos's work on Christian naming ceremonies was thought provoking, and I will reflect more on his concept of the 'embryonic potency of an identity' (p. 280). Bissell provides a helpful overview of a whole-church response to abuse which is supportive and which encompasses the notion of the healing circle.

With such a book there are always chapters that one will be more drawn to than others, but there is sufficient material here to encourage those involved in the education of children at whatever level to read it and reflect on what insights you have gained that will change practice. I have certainly been transformed by the notion of a playful wisdom.

Sally Nash

JECB 18:1 (2014): 104–6   1366-5456

Emma Long
The Church-State Debate: Religion, Education and the Establishment Clause in Post War America
New York: Continuum, 2012 hb 280pp $120.00
ISBN 978-1-4411-3446-2

The First Amendment to the US Constitution begins, "Congress shall make no law respecting an establishment of religion, or prohibiting the free exercise thereof; or abridging the freedom of speech, or of the press; or the right of the people peaceably to assemble, and to petition the Government for a redress of grievances." Emma Long employs a historical approach to analyze fifty years of Supreme Court rulings pertaining to Establishment Clause jurisprudence. She asserts that rulings which seem "incoherent and inconsistent, lacking an overall structure and failing to provide clear guidance about the proper relationship between church and state" (p. 8), can be better understood when viewed through a framework of legal theory and the broader historical context that have had impacts on the decisions.

Focusing on debates and court cases involving schools and education policy, Long organizes the text around three main areas of controversy. The first, school aid, examines rulings pertaining to the provision of government benefits to religious schools and their students. From the 1947 *Everson v. Board of Education* ruling, which permitted reimbursement for religious school costs, to the 1997 *Agostini v. Felton* decision, which permitted remedial education services for economically disadvantaged children to take place on religious school grounds, Long skillfully weaves together context and issue to provide the reader with a historical framework for understanding these rulings.

Long's second section on school prayer begins with a brief history of "battles over prayer and Bible reading" (p. 83) traced to the Irish immigration in the late 1830s. Chapters 4, 5, and 6 discuss religion and education immediately after World War II and school prayer rulings during the Reagan era, ending with the Rehnquist court's reassessment. School prayer debate in the second half of the twentieth century reflects the court's efforts to reconcile the important place of faith in the lives of many Americans with constitutional safeguards against establishment of religion. "Despite internal challenges and external pressures, the basic principle that public schools and their staff may not support, endorse, or encourage religious exercise or practices during the school day or at other school events has endured" (p. 153).

In the third section, Long reviews the court's interactions in the area of equal access, noting philosophical disagreements existing within the court. Divisions present in 1947 were still evident some fifty years later, mirroring broad disagreements in American society surrounding the place of religion and its role in the nation's schools.

In the concluding chapter, Long points out that the court has consistently refused to adhere to any one theory, considering instead the issues and context surrounding school aid, school prayer, and equal access. Recognizing the inherent differences in these areas enlightens the reader, refuting the oversimplified viewpoint that casts the court as unable to chart a clear course or develop a consistent structure through which to view church-state issues. Long asserts that court cases cannot be understood separately from their contexts. While legal factors are foundational to church-state relations, they are only part of the broader view necessary for a historical understanding.

Long's text is not light reading, but she does present her findings in a way that a person not well versed in legal matters can understand. Perhaps most valuable are the succinct and readable summaries of the key issues. These provide lay readers such as myself with a concise and understandable review of the issues at hand. *The Church-State Debate* would serve well as a supplemental text in a school law course or other preparatory course for American school administrators. Issues governed by the Establishment Clause are encountered in public school settings on a daily basis. This historical approach, which considers societal and economic factors as well as legal rulings, presents critical information in an understandable way.

Karen Maxwell

JECB 18:1 (2014): 106–9   1366-5456

Roger Lundin (ed.)
Christ across the Disciplines: Past, Present, Future
Grand Rapids, MI: Eerdmans, 2013 pb 232pp $20.00
ISBN 978-0-8028-6947-0

Christ across the Disciplines presents the lectures from a year-long series celebrating Wheaton College's sesquicentennial. Roger Lundin acknowledges Arthur Holmes's influence in the integration of faith and learning, and these essays seek to further such work, their authors coming from a variety of theological and national backgrounds.

David Bebbington examines the interrelation of history and faith since 1900 and notes that historians 'do not come to their evidence with blank minds, analyzing data with the detachment of computers. Rather, historians are shaped by their fundamental beliefs' (p. 17). He says that the 1960s were a period preoccupied with economic history, with historians, whether of the right or the left, being influenced by the prestige of science. Since then the postmodernist approach has changed the state of play, and Bebbington evaluates the positives and negatives of such an approach.

John Schmalzbauer recounts the creative tensions among evangelicals in academic life in the United States, which I found interesting reading, as someone from the other side of the Atlantic. The backgrounds of key figures are examined, as are their aims, struggles, and faults. Commenting on the present situation in the States, where 'few Americans have regular contact with those who think differently from themselves', Schmalzbauer says that 'evangelical scholars may be different. Positioned between a conservative religious subculture and an academy that leans to the left, they have frequent interchange with both sides of the political spectrum' (p. 71).

David Livingstone examines science and religion and his article is aided by numerous historical examples. He warns that

> we, too, are located; and, if history is anything to go by, we are all too apt to mistake the particular for the transcendental, cultural forms for theological principles, contingency for necessity. For that reason faith traditions, if they are to remain vibrant rather than moribund, need to be in constant, critical dialogue with themselves. (pp. 98–99)

Livingstone's article says that science-faith encounters cannot be simply reduced to conflict or cooperation, and he argues for the significance of the place where interactions between science and faith are made, as well as the political and rhetorical utility of various scientific theories.

John Webster wrote an essay on the theology of the intellectual life, and the following quotation was probably the greatest surprise for me in the whole book:

> We have grown accustomed to consider curiosity either innocent or virtuous. For the earlier Christian tradition, however, curiosity is a vice. It is vicious because it is a corruption of the virtue of *studiousness*. (p. 109)

He argues that curiosity applies the intellect to improper objects, attempts to know reality without acknowledging the creator, has a craving for novelty, and pursues knowledge improperly, for example, to increase self-esteem. He argues that regenerated intellectuals know that their intellectual existence has been converted, are teachable, require the use of moral and intellectual virtues, calmly embrace situational limitations and opportunities, and study created things 'in order to ascend to contemplation of God' (p. 115).

Regarding the postmodern challenge, Eleonore Stump argues that 'we ought to reject postmodernism and retain the hope of modernism that there is one truth that holds universally for all human beings'. However, as a counterbalance to this she says that 'human evil has the power to warp understanding in the service of self-interest. The only safety here is to join ranks with the postmodernists and welcome diverse perspectives, especially those critical of our own' (p. 128). She also wishes to uphold a distinction between orthodoxy and heresy, but one which does not reject the holder of heretical views.

Stephen Barr looks at modern physics, and in response to the claim that science has debunked many ideas in the last century, argues that 'what it chiefly debunked . . . was the materialist's old "story of science"' (p. 142) and uses the big bang theory, quantum mechanics, and anthropic coincidences as evidence against a materialist position.

Jeremy Begbie examines the Reformed theological position's role in the arts and argues for, among other points, 'a re-formed vision of beauty for the arts: insofar as it refuses to marginalize the cross and all that is implicated there, it *spurns sentimentality*' (p. 160). He also warns of a sacramentality that conceives of a divine presence as one of 'bland infinitude' rather than the active covenanting God of Israel (p. 167). He wishes to see the arts 'articulating depths of the Word of the gospel and our experience of it that are otherwise unheard or unfelt, while nonetheless being responsible and faithful to the normative texts of the faith' (p. 181).

Katherine Clay Bassard reflects upon conversations about race. She comments that reconciliation and reparations are two terms used in racial discourse and focus on human acts, but that 'redemption is a God act. Moreover, redemption gives us a language that allows us to view history within a field of hope and radical change' (p. 189), and it is a concept which Bassard uses to explore the work of three authors of neo-slave narratives.

In the final chapter, Sujit Sivasundaram makes a case that the concepts of race, culture, and nation have a Christian inheritance, which valued both unity and diversity. He studies three figures from the nineteenth century, one for each concept, noting the complexities involved in these Christians' thinking. Regarding the last of the three concepts, he writes that we should be *transnational* 'not in the sense of throwing out the idea of the nation, but in the sense of decontextualizing it within a conversation that is more mutually respectful, open, and global' (p. 224).

My only question is why the book is entitled 'Christ *across the Disciplines*', as the person of Christ does not feature significantly in the majority of the essays—the title should thus not lead people to conclude that all the essays are overtly Christological. Having said this, I do not wish to detract from the standard of the essays, and would commend the book in addressing a diversity of disciplines and how they interact with Christian faith.

Andrew C. Palfreyman

JECB 18:1 (2014): 109–11   1366-5456

Guglielmo Malizia and Sergio Cicatelli
The Catholic School under Scrutiny:
Ten Years of Research in Italy (1998–2008)
Bern: Peter Lang, 2011 pb 247pp $150.84/€62.40
ISBN 978-3-0343-0558-7

The introduction describes the authors' intent to document the evolution and subsequent decade of work completed by the Study Centre for Catholic Schools (CSSC) in Italy. It should be noted that the authors are stakeholders in the success of the CSSC venture. Malizia was the CSSC director and dean of the Faculty of Education at the partner university (Salesian University) for the first decade of CSSC operations. He has since received an extended contract to continue as director while the CSSC undergoes review and restructure. Cicatelli is a researcher for the CSSC, principal of an Italian Catholic school, and consultant for the Italian Ministry of Education.

There are nine chapters and three sections, as well as an appendix listing all publications of the CSSC since 1998. The first section reviews the development of the CSSC, the identity and role of all constituents, and the professional program of the CSSC described in three work plans, and it offers a positive assessment of the impact of the CSSC on Italian Catholic schools. This section is very detailed and would most interest someone studying the educational history of Italy. Its broader audience appeal is limited, in my opinion.

Chapter 2 discusses the identity of the Catholic school and its dual role to communicate "knowledge-truth . . . (on the faith-culture side) and values . . . (on the faith-life side)" (p. 57). This discussion is revisited and extended throughout the text, offering an opportunity for any school to consider its mission and purpose within a broader conversation about the function of education.

Chapter 5, section 2, "Evangelisation, Religious Education and

Religious Teaching," addresses the unexpected discovery of a division between teaching Catholic religion as academic content and teaching the Catholic faith. The "interaction between religious teaching and the teaching of the Catholic religion, or more particularly between scholastic teaching and catechesis" and particularly pedagogical issues of instructional approach and assessment/evaluation practices (p. 87) are addressed. The authors also examine a general failure to embrace evangelical aims in Catholic schools and offer suggestions for energizing the schools' evangelical mission while warning that by failing to act on their evangelistic responsibilities, the "qualification 'Catholic' [becomes] more or less nominal" (p. 94).

Chapter 8, on the condition of the student, was the most applicable to a general audience. Descriptions of "children of the media" or the "bed generation" (a generation that lives closed up in its bedroom, communicating with the outside world by way of new information and communication technology) and their frustrations with increasing social violence, reduced opportunities for employment and personal advancement, and an adult world that is often disappointing (pp. 160–61) are not unique to Italy's youth. However, differences in worldview expressed by Italian Catholic school students versus their public school peers were novel to this reviewer. Survey data show that Catholic school students are generally happier with their present lives and future potential, feel more capable of handling the challenges of the adult world, are more satisfied in their personal and familial relationships, are less prone to risk-taking behaviors, and are more service oriented in their conceptualization of their civic responsibilities (pp. 167–68). They report deeper religious affiliation; they have better articulated understanding of the personal, social, and cultural significance of religion; and they demonstrate more consistent and sincere practiced faith than their peers (p. 168). Cicatelli enumerates the "protective factors" the Catholic school offers to explain these outcomes, including closer teacher-student relationships and personalized education.

Throughout, the authors strive to identify what is unique and significant about the Catholic school. The answer appears to lie less in the study of Catholic religion and more in how the Catholic faith infuses the school culture and its concern with the "diversity and unrepeatability of each pupil/person" (p. 221) in order to differentiate for each a unique educational program and experience. This philosophy is shared by teachers and school managers and is seen in the culture of welcome, acceptance, and love communicated to community members that seeks nothing less than the "transforming of society" as its aim (p. 225). This book offers a strong beginning argument for ways that faith-based education can inform every interaction that occurs in the school setting for the benefit of its members.

The final chapter anticipates CSSC's future, including ideas for its next contributions to the development of Catholic education in Italy. My concern with this book is its limited audience appeal given its geographical specificity. However, there are elements of the book, including those discussed in this review, that provide avenues for reflection and discussion for anyone interested in promoting faith-based education throughout the world.

Lisa Laurier

JECB 18:1 (2014): 111–13   1366-5456

Noel Merino (ed.)
Introducing Issues with Opposing Viewpoints:
Religion in Schools
Farmington Hills, MI: Greenhaven Press, 2012 pb 122pp $37.00
ISBN 978-0-7377-5685-2

True to its aim, *Religion in Schools* gives its reader an authentic lens from which to view the controversial issues of religion that affect public schools today. This *Introducing Issues with Opposing Viewpoints* volume clearly meets its goal of "open[ing] readers' minds to the critically divergent views that comprise our world's most important debates" (p. 5), in this case, the debate regarding religion's place in public schools. A relatively short read (the three chapters span less than 100 pages), this revised edition is highly engaging and aesthetically appealing, making it an excellent resource. I found Merino's book to be easy to read (its audience is adolescents in grades 7 through 10), but I would never describe it as a simplistic text.

Merino's hand in editing the chapters of this book helps the reader to embrace the notion that "debate is what 'shape[s] our society and drive[s] it forward'" (p. 5). Quite simply, this book provides us with a framework for wholesome debate by sharing perspectives from those experts and authorities in the field who play major roles in interpreting the intentions of the framers of the First Amendment and ensuring that the public's rights under the First Amendment are protected. Three major questions are addressed in this text: Should religion be allowed in public schools? Should alternatives to evolution be taught in public schools? Should religious activities be allowed in public schools?

This book clearly substantiated for me the power of an informed truth when thinking critically and pragmatically about the most significant issues of religion that public schools face today. It brings to light the work of individuals such as Charles Haynes, Oliver Thomas, and Congressman Robert C. Byrd, as well as that of advocacy groups such as the American Atheists. It introduced me to a range of different views that I had never considered. The colorful "Fast Fact" boxes, graphics, and illustrations meaningfully engaged me with the content I was reading. Indeed, it was this volume's design and structure that made me feel as though the information was flowing from the page.

To ensure that I was critically synthesizing the "perspectives" shared by experts in the field, each chapter began with a brief synopsis of the pages to come, along with a set of response-to-text questions to facilitate my own critical inquiry into each viewpoint. At the end of each argument I read, I was challenged further with evaluating questions to help me either expand upon or compare and contrast what I was learning as I continued to read each perspective. Finally, in addition to the annotated bibliography that was provided at the end of the book, I especially appreciated the comprehensive list of agency/organization addresses and website information that could be used for further investigation of primary sources.

What I appreciated most about this book was the rainbow of perspectives representing each of the longstanding controversial questions of religion's impact on teaching and learning in public schools. I was pleasantly surprised to find more than the typical two-sides-of-the-coin debate. Rather, each chapter presented perspectives representing a continuum of opinions that were derived from each individual's first-hand experiences. Alone, each color of the rainbow is just a color, but together the colors of the rainbow make it one of the most beautiful sights we see. We can view the debate of religion in schools in a similar way.

This book appeals to a large audience. Adults of all ages who want to be informed about the First Amendment would gain much from this anthology. Those who would most benefit from its content include parents of young children, high school students, teacher candidates, and public school teachers and administrators who want to inform their practice. I especially envision this text being included as a component of study in religious education youth groups and high school debate courses. Its design and organizational structure also make it an engaging and meaningful text for high school government and history courses, cross-studies liberal arts courses, foundational education courses in teacher preparation programs (both Christian and secular), and professional development workshops.

I highly recommend this book because of the knowledge one will gain about the longstanding issues central to the First Amendment, the Establishment Clause, and the Free Exercise Clause. The readers of this book will gain invaluable information and find it to be a valuable reference tool as well.

Diana D. Abbott

JECB 18:1 (2014): 113–15   1366-5456

S. Parker, R. Freathy, and L. J. Francis (eds.)
Religious Education and Freedom of Religion and Belief
New York: Peter Lang, 2012 hb 275pp $65.00
ISBN 978-3034307543

There are a number of questions scholars, students, and other readers professionally concerned with religious education are likely to ask themselves when considering whether or not to purchase a particular book, such as its focus, what it intends to achieve, and its relevance for the intended audience. A book reviewer ponders similar questions, and in this particular case they pose particular difficulties.

This is volume two in the series published by Peter Lang entitled Religion, Education and Values, an edited collection of conference papers. Religious education and freedom of religion and belief was the theme of the seventeenth International Seminar on Religious Education and Values, from which the thirteen papers in this book derive.

The thematic choice was, we are told, a deliberate attempt by researchers to influence policy makers, practitioners, and learners. As interesting as it may be to practitioners, however, I am not convinced that the collection is likely either to reach or to exert much general influence on such a diverse audience as the editors might wish. Nevertheless, there is much to be admired, though the quality of the historical, theoretical, and empirical perspectives on such a wide-ranging topic varies considerably. Many were excellent, intriguing, enlightening, and intellectually stimulating; others less so.

But that is often the case when chapters come from different authors, and, because of its particular genesis, taken as a whole, I found the book a little disappointing. It is not a comprehensive survey of the field—how could it be?—nor does it provide the coverage expected of a student reader. It would be invidious, however, to dwell too much upon the perhaps personal perceptions on this reviewer.

The first four papers deal with the twin concepts of freedom *of* religion and *from* religion, highlighting particular dilemmas arising from the diverse, pluralistic nature of a variety of Western-style liberal democracies. I found particularly interesting Freathy and Parker's case study of the Birmingham Agreed Syllabus for Religious Education, charting the influence of Harry Stopes-Roe, Harold J. Blackman, and the British Humanist Association on Religious Education in the 1960s and '70s. Given the purpose of the paper, the authors' decision to exclude any reference to the role of voluntary aided Church sector—particularly Roman Catholic— in its formulation is completely understandable, though to define such schools as not being 'fully maintained' is to misunderstand the technical and legal meaning of the term. It is interesting to note that the relevant Catholic authorities were fully involved in the Birmingham SACRE and the development of the syllabus. The irony is that it was not authorized for use in Catholic schools.

The same concepts are explored in the six theoretical perspectives contained in the second section of the book. Jeff Astley's analysis of the differences between them is, as usual with this writer, clear, incisive, and well worth absorbing, as is Mario D'Souza's exploration of basic principles which would allow the flourishing of religious diversity, and forms of religious education designed to support and maintain different religious traditions within a stable pluralistic society.

The third and shortest section, featuring just three papers, is for me as a practitioner the least satisfactory; not so much for the quality of the contributions but the paucity of (apparently) suitable contributions. Jan Grajczonek's paper, a report on a quantitative study of teacher-pupil interaction in a Catholic school, highlighted the practical difficulties facing religious educators working in 'confessional' schools serving a community having a variety of faith backgrounds. His illustration of the ways in which such teachers can ignore the diversity of religio-cultural backgrounds of their pupils should become compulsory reading for trainee religious educators.

Unfortunately, this fascinating paper highlights an important missing element in this volume; namely, an exploration of confessional religious education within schools serving a particular religious community. The Catholic Church is the largest non-governmental agency providing education worldwide. Their schools appear to be popular and successful in meeting the educational and social aspirations of many parents. The many religious educators that work in such institutions would find little in this volume to help develop their understanding of their educative role and their obligations toward their subject, the parents, and the children whom they serve.

It seems churlish to end by criticizing the editors for this book's omissions rather than to stress its merits; and it has many. But while the omissions can be understood—you can only select from the papers that are submitted—they will limit the potential audience. And that is a pity.

Andrew Morris

JECB 18:1 (2014): 115–17   1366-5456

Mark A. Pike
Mere Education. C. S. Lewis as Teacher for Our Time
Cambridge: Lutterworth, 2013 pb 200pp £17.50
ISBN 978-0-7188-9325-5

In this much-needed work, Mark A. Pike makes an effort to present C. S. Lewis's view on education and schooling to parents, teachers, and leaders to help them to defend schools "from the incoming tide of ideological assumptions that threaten to erode and undermine the wholeness and purity of education" (p. 12). The author has produced a superb work, synthesizing the thought on education and schooling sprinkled through many of Lewis's books—fiction and nonfiction, apologetic, and purely academic. In other words, the book has been written to "inspire excellence in teaching, leadership, the curriculum and assessment by helping readers attend to the foundations of education and schooling" (p. 12).

The book is organized in four parts, each consisting of three chapters. Part 1, entitled "The Hinge of the Wardrobe Door," underlines the relevance of values education at home and in schools. Pike defends the legitimacy of Christian schools and points to the need for younger generations to have contact with "what the Christians say" (quoting Lewis, p. 39). The second part, "The Furniture of the House," refers to some key concepts and contents of schooling: liberal (holistic) education, sex education, and biblical education. After reading chapter 6, I would rather it were entitled "Biblical Literacy" because it is devoted to students' acquaintance with the Bible as a literary work, not with the learning and embodiment of its teaching. The third part, "Lewis as Cultural Interpreter for Educators," introduces three current issues: cultural, citizenship, and democratic education. The last part, "The Professor's House," addresses teacher and leadership education, and the future of education.

The organization of the book makes it very readable. Every chapter is introduced by a summary of the previous one, with an example or a conceptual clarification. Then the author presents what Lewis has to say about issues related to the theme of the chapter. Pike turns to Lewis's work and quotes him extensively. However, some quotations are too short for readers to understand the whole idea. Each chapter finishes by anticipating the theme of the next one and offering a study guide. This is a good idea. However, many questions are too tied to the respective chapter's text and are somewhat schoolbook questions or far from practice. The book includes notes, bibliography, and two useful indexes: a Scripture index and a general one.

The more successful chapters are, in my opinion, the first one, about character education, and the tenth, devoted to teacher education. This last one has made me ask myself several questions. Among them are: To what extent do I enact the qualities of an excellent teacher? To what extent do I promote real dialogue in my classes? Do I ask "real" questions to my students?

I will pose just a few questions related to three controversial issues risen by Pike, although the book addresses many more: the place of the welfare state, the definition of leadership, and who controls our Western societies. Is the dismantling of the welfare state in the name of economic stability not detrimental to the poor and the excluded, and does it not primarily benefit banks, big businesses, and the rich? Perhaps it should be said that I am writing from south continental Europe, where the current economic crisis is having severe consequences in many people's daily lives. Is hierarchical leadership the best way to think and act in educational organizations, or is there a place for more horizontal models and distributed leadership? To what extent are *"the controllers"* no longer state experts but different kinds of pressure groups (economic, social, political, or religious) and supranational agents (for example, different decision-making levels in the European Union, or the OECD)? Pike uses *the controllers* as synonymous with Lewis's *conditioners* in *The Abolition of Man*.

The language, the notes, and the structure of the book lead me to think Pike intended his book more for teachers than for parents. Parents who do read it will likely be those very interested in the subject, those fond of Lewis, or those with a university degree. Undoubtedly the book will be very helpful for students of education. I fear, however, that it will attract mainly people who consider Lewis to be an authority as a Christian.

Pike's contribution is relevant, but I contend that "mere Christianity" is one thing and "mere education" is another. It can be argued that Pike's reading of Lewis has not let him arrive at "mere education" because Lewis wrote on education in many of his books but not in a systematic way, as it was the case with *Mere Christianity*.

Moreover, I think there is more freedom in developing a Christian view on mere education than in developing a view of mere Christianity. In dealing with Christianity, there are some nonnegotiable issues clearly revealed in Scripture, most of them properly treated by Lewis in his *Mere Christianity*. But as we speak and reflect on education, we are applying biblical principles, which in several contexts may have different embodiments.

In spite of the criticisms I have made, Christian educators will grow in their understanding of teaching and their development as teachers from reading Pike's book. The book will also be very useful in every Christian institution of higher education as a valuable tool for promoting reflection and action in education from a Christian stance.

Pablo Bonilla Santana

JECB 18:1 (2014): 118–20   1366-5456

Todd C. Ream and Perry L Glanzer
The Idea of a Christian College:
A Reexamination for Today's University
Eugene, OR: Cascade Books, 2013 pb 158pp $18.00
ISBN 978-1-61097-327-3

This is not the first time Ream and Glanzer have written together. In fact, generous elements of the central arguments of this reexamination have been shared elsewhere (for example, in their 2007 volume, *Christian Faith and Scholarship* and *An Exploration of Contemporary Debates*). Their collaboration this time was written to honor Arthur F. Holmes, long-time professor of philosophy at Wheaton College and author of a groundbreaking 1975 book by the same title. Holmes's book became required reading for many undergraduate students and almost all new faculty joining a Protestant, faith-based institution. And although he didn't coin the phrase "the integration of faith and learning," Holmes is the person most associated with it, now a recognizable code word and slogan for the Christian college. The authors are to be congratulated for remembering and recognizing Arthur Holmes's teaching and writing, and for honoring his legacy and influence on Christian higher education.

Writing to students, faculty, and administrators in faith-based institutions, the authors rightly point out that much has changed in Christian higher education since 1975. They point to three things: the changing nature of worship and the church, a more developed understanding of what it means to be fully human, and the rise of the Christian university. While their reexamination is roughly organized to shadow the chapters of the original volume and each chapter starts with a quotation from Holmes, it is these three major changes that frame the arguments presented. The book moves thoughtfully, combining theological and philosophical arguments with real-life stories and campus examples, making it accessible and inviting. However, although the cover suggests that this would be good reading for all first-year students in Christian colleges, the arguments are more applicable to graduate students, faculty, and administrators. And the book has a certain Reformed orientation, much like Holmes's original. Persons from other traditions (Wesleyan, Anabaptist, Quaker, etc.) will find the recurring focus on reforming and redeeming learning, learners, teaching, curriculum, institutions, disciplines, professions, cocurricular activities, and almost everything else to be a bit wearisome at times. Those from the Reformed tradition, however, should feel right at home with this description of the Christian mandate.

Ream and Glanzer argue forcefully for the centrality of corporate worship as the shaping centerpiece of institution life. This ecclesial emphasis was not addressed by Holmes in 1975, and the authors worry that the absence of corporate worship today signals trouble for any institution that names Christ, particularly so given the move of many Christian colleges to minimize or cancel altogether their chapel services. On the other hand, if the intent is, indeed, to make disciples and promote spiritual formation, very few pastors would suggest that the way to do so in their congregations would be to add another worship service. Many institutions are looking to more small-group-oriented activities to achieve the goal of spiritual formation. This book offers a timely reminder of the importance of worship and it pushes the conversation forward with a serious caution.

The second major change Ream and Glanzer address is our developing understanding of what it means to be human and the continuing importance of attending to the formation of the whole person. Particularly in this age of specialization (not something specifically addressed by Holmes), this book is a crucial reminder of the importance of vocation and calling, the necessity of wise friends and mentors on campus, and the significance and consequence of finding our identity in Christ. On campus, we are reminded of the interconnection and mutually supportive nature of cocurricular and classroom activities.

The third change since 1975 is the emergence of the Christian university with the addition of professional programs, graduate students, and an emphasis on the discovery of new knowledge (scholarship). Certainly in 1975, Holmes had the liberal arts college in mind (perhaps with Wheaton as a model, given that he worked there), while Ream and Glanzer have in mind the Christian university (perhaps Baylor, since they both have appointments there). Their emphasis on the Christian university continues a yeasty conversation about the role, nature, and demands of Christian scholarship in our institutions. It should be noted that there are really very few Christian research (R1) institutions. As the authors noted, just calling yourself a university does not make you one. Honestly, most Christian colleges and universities have neither the money nor the mission to become

R1 institutions. While the few (Baylor and Notre Dame, to name two) serve legitimate purposes, I wonder whether the focus on the Christian research university is prudent. Clearly most Christian colleges and universities are teaching institutions. Perhaps it is better to think of Christian institutions as T1—transformational institutions—whose mission is to teach, to shape, and to send rather than to produce new knowledge. A yeasty conversation, indeed!

Ream and Glanzer set out to honor Arthur Holmes, to update the consideration of Christian higher education given major changes since 1975, and to focus attention on the importance of corporate worship, the consideration of the whole person, and the emergence of the Christian university. In that effort, they have been successful. I recommend this book to all advanced students, faculty, and administrators learning and serving in faith-based institutions. Ream and Glanzer have faithfully pushed the conversation forward. Now it is up to each of us to join the conversation, too.

Patrick Allen

JECB 18:1 (2014): 120–22   1366-5456

Geir Skeie, Judith Everington, Ina ter Avest, and Siebren Miedema (eds.)
Exploring Context in Religious Education Research: Empirical, Methodological and Theoretical Perspectives
Münster: Waxmann, 2013 pb 272pp €32.90
ISBN 978-3-8309-2902-4

Academic study of religious education in public schools is more prominent in Europe than some other countries, including Canada. The European discussion is partially informed by the European Network for Religious Education in Europe through Contextual Approaches (ENRECA), which produced this edited volume of essays on research in religious education. As European countries become more religiously and socio-culturally diverse, the contexts in which religious education research is conducted are also more complex. As increasing diversity is not unique to Europe, this book has much to offer anyone interested in religion and education.

The introduction directs the reader to read the last chapter first, where

Geir Skeie argues for the object-context relationship to be more systematically integrated in research. Skeie stresses the "triadic interrelationship between socio-cultural surroundings, research process and research object" (pp. 255–56) and calls for contextual religious education research "to account for the relationship between descriptive knowledge about context and the normative acts of persons in the field" (p. 265). He supports research approaches that open up communication between the researcher and practitioner, because the latter also contextualizes. In short, Skeie suggests a "double contextualisation" process in which researchers place the research object within a particular cultural and social setting, accounting for the relationship between the object and the setting, and remain cognizant of the human action embedded in the research object. In this manner the research project itself is a context.

The first section of the book is comprised of six empirical studies, all of which interact with Skeie's double contextualization to some degree. I highlight two chapters that reveal the importance of context for research and education. Dag Husebø focuses on the participatory trajectories, or instigated negotiations, of participants in a practice-oriented collaborative research project between teacher educators, student teachers, and teachers in a Norwegian religious education class. The research provided new knowledge about the context of teacher education and educational research. Specifically, the teachers asked to be involved in the theoretical lectures given to the student teachers and to develop their own teaching projects. In light of the teacher requests, researchers recognized that they, and Norwegian teacher education programs in general, did not initially perceive the teachers as learners.

In another chapter, Trine Anker conceptualizes context as network. Following the French philosopher Bruno Latour, Anker views objects as actors within a network, and context as the movement between actors. In schools, rules are objects, and when frozen at a moment in time can be represented on a poster in a classroom. Anker observed a grade 6 and a grade 7 classroom, each with two sandwich toasters. The toasters became sites of contention, in one class leading to teacher-imposed rules, student reactions, and the creation of new rules. While the teacher in the other class did not create specific rules, toaster use was determined by popularity. In both classes the objects of toasters and rules changed the contexts of the classrooms and the meaning construction occurring within them. Anker further discussed how context as network accounted for changed teacher and student practices due to the presence of the researcher.

The second part of the book addresses methodological and theoretical perspectives. Authors delineate various approaches to religious education, discuss the contexts of policy regarding religious education in Europe, and investigate whether the inclusion of religious education in social studies in Sweden affects central RE knowledge. Another develops a value "model of context based on students' life-experiences" (p. 214) that impact student conceptions of faith. Still another examines context within a comparative methodology comprised of the three dimensions of supranational, national, and sub-national processes.

Most of the chapters in this book are quite theoretical, with the authors drawing from a variety of theoretical traditions. The diversity of engagement with Skeie's research challenge offers a rich exploration of context. On the one hand, these theoretical and research foci limit the audience to academics. On the other hand, the six empirical studies occurred in K–12 classrooms and are valuable reads for both educators and those involved in teacher preparation. In addition, various chapters provide initial thoughts of how to think about the religious life and practices of a school. As Oddrun Marie Hovde Bråten demonstrates, religious contexts are present in all schools and shape the manner in which students experience the curriculum, regardless of whether the contexts are overtly discussed or even acknowledged. Given the breadth of stakeholder interests reflected in the various research topics, the book is of value to anyone interested in the nature and role of religion in education.

Margie Patrick

JECB 18:1 (2014): 122–24   1366-5456

R. J. Snell and Steven D. Cone
Authentic Cosmopolitanism:
Love, Sin, and Grace in the Christian University
Eugene, OR: Pickwick, 2013 pb 190pp $16.00
ISBN 978-1-61097-365-6

Snell and Cone see their work as "contributing to the literature on Christian higher education, pulling in the same direction as others attempting to go beyond pedagogies captured by an anthropology of the thinking being" (p. 169). Specifically, they build on the foundation laid by James Smith in *Desiring the Kingdom* (Grand Rapids, MI: Baker Academic, 2009) to focus even more deliberately on intentionality and love. The overall thesis of the book is that the purpose of Christian higher education is to educate students "towards the goal of self-transcending love," something they call "authentic cosmopolitanism" (p. 181). Their study is carefully crafted to allow philosophical conversations between both ancient and more contemporary voices, thus synthesizing quite a bit of scholarly thought on the topics of intentionality and love. Each section builds upon the previous one, and each chapter flows logically from the one that precedes it.

First, the authors explore an anthropology of love that draws upon Plato, Augustine, and Aquinas and then turn to Martin Heidegger and Charles Taylor in order to define a key term and an area of deliberate focus: authenticity. Here, as elsewhere in the book, the authors are careful to address the concerns of possible critics, explaining that their use of the term "authentic" is not postmodern in connotation but rather fully engaging "with the world of value, meaning, and self-transcendence" (p. 64). The authors then explore the interaction of Bernard Lonergan with the other voices, relying heavily upon Lonergan's theories to make their claims. It is Lonergan who offers "a phenomenology of the concrete subject based in the primacy of the human subject as a loving, desiring being" (p. 66). He does so in part by addressing the need for religious conversion, acknowledging that humans cannot achieve their own self-transcendence apart from the grace of God. Cone and Snell then discuss the debilitating effects of sin—especially the ways in which bias distorts everything—and the necessary appropriation of grace, adding the voices of Maslow and Piaget to the ongoing conversation. The last section examines the importance of value ethics, contrasting it to other popular types of ethics, and then turns toward defining another key term: cosmopolitanism. In summary, for Snell and Cone, authentic cosmopolitanism—the goal of Christian higher education—is "authentic subjectivity attained through intellectual, moral, and religious conversion" (p. 150).

The authors offer several disclaimers, explaining that they are not making any attempt toward practical suggestions for how the theoretical concepts they are exploring might play out in Christian universities. They also explicitly state that the "book is intended for a serious and educated readership, but not for specialists" (p. xi). As someone who considers herself to fit that description, I have a mixed reaction. There were moments when I wished that I had more background knowledge in philosophy, especially on Bernard Lonergan. Frankly, not being a specialist puts me—and others like me—at a bit of a disadvantage since I must then rely on the authors' interpretation and opinion of Lonergan's works. In other words, without exploring Lonergan myself I cannot decide with any integrity whether or not what the authors are proposing is valid for me or for Christian higher education as I see it. On the other hand, there are also sections in the book when Cone and Snell used illustrations that were readily understandable to me to unpack complex philosophical ideas. Specifically, they use the family or oxygen as a way of explaining how the real world is "mediated to us by a set of meanings" (p. 70) and the character of Sydney Carton in Charles Dickens's novel *A Tale of Two Cities* to illustrate different types of ethics related to decision making. When they used such devices, the material became much more accessible to me.

Overall, I believe this work to have achieved its purpose; it does contribute to the ongoing conversation about Christian higher education as it has turned toward educating for desire. In particular, it explores a philosophical underpinning in fresh and interesting ways. And as much as some of us would like to know more about what this might look like more concretely in our classrooms and on our campuses, we should be grateful to Snell and Cone for the hard work they have done to provide a scholarly foundation for the shift we may be engaged in creating.

Laurie R. Matthias

JECB 18:1 (2014): 124–26   1366-5456

Ryan N. S. Topping
Happiness and Wisdom: Augustine's Early Theology of Education
Washington, DC: Catholic University of America Press, 2012
hb 252pp $58.00
ISBN 978-0-8132-1973-8

Ryan N. S. Topping begins with a brief description of ancient liberal arts education and its schema. He concentrates on Augustine's early work, which was directed toward the educational mission of the church. It is within this historical and philosophical context that Augustine eschews his early epistemology of education. Significant for education, which seems most relevant to this writer, are Topping's descriptions of Augustine's view of Curriculum and Ciceronian Skepticism. These two areas are at the heart of the educational struggle of our day. The more the progressive empiricist tries to quantify and align all teachers everywhere, the greater the noise of disagreement will grow. Topping has touched the very heart of the issue in *Happiness and Wisdom* and gives voice to an alternative that is reasonable and educationally proven.

Topping shows the contrast between the purpose of education in Augustine's day and our day. The divergence of contrast could not be greater. Augustine viewed education as a means to heal the soul. The purpose is to find happiness, virtue, and community among believers. Modern education views the purpose of education as a vehicle to promote societal values or perhaps more realistically economic gain. Augustine saw liberal arts as windows to eternity, whereas modern education sees education as a tool for gain. Curriculum was more than a need to learn for learning's sake alone. Augustine viewed this as a turning inward with no real purpose at all. He proposed that happiness is man's orientation, and without a deeper commitment toward God and virtue, learning would become pessimistic and hopeless.

Augustine's Curriculum encouraged and fostered virtue in the student, whether toward man or God. He would have the student turn his gaze toward inner man and toward Christ. Augustine would define curriculum as the study of text, the study of concepts, or a sequence of activities. The teacher and the student will need to draw boundaries around the curriculum, and thus selection becomes paramount. Therefore, one of the key purposes is to define boundaries. For Augustine the curriculum would start with linguistics and proceed to the mathematical disciplines. Topping gives voice to the real issue of education today. In contrast to the progressive empiricist, the goal is not being number one in the world in a set of tests but rather how man can be virtuous and seek God.

The skepticism of our day or that of Augustine's day will still undermine the certitude of life. As Augustine said, "It was like searching for treasure, without knowing if there was any treasure at all" (p. 92). He taught that a student should not give up hope of seeking the truth. Men should use prayer in the belief that God will listen and that both avenues would lead to the Almighty.

In Augustine's battle with the Manichean Dualist, defining good versus evil was a major impasse. The dualist had two sides and perhaps three: good, bad, and neutral. Topping illustrates that in Augustine, defining evil was simply a lack of good. Thus, the liberal arts would really have the purpose of leading us back to God. Augustine's approach was not so much the proper mix of faith and reason as it was the proper approach to faith and authority. Topping quotes John Dewey as saying that "learning has meant, on the whole, piling up, worshipping, and holding fast to what is handed down from the past with the title of knowledge" (p. 173). Topping concludes that Dewey is saying, "Do not trust authority but choose independent inquiry as the means to knowledge. Therefore, approach knowledge from the scientific method rather than faith in authority and tradition."

Happiness and Wisdom is very useful for a wide range of readers. Educators need to have a second view of education's purpose or at least to compare the two views. Skepticism and defeatism will deteriorate the attitudes of students and supporters of our institutions. Topping has contributed to a debate that is age-old yet culturally relevant today. Happiness, virtue, and community were the purposes of the liberal arts education for Augustine; now Topping has let us hear him.

Joseph Olson

JECB 18:1 (2014): 126–28   1366-5456

Carolyn Weber

Holy Is the Day: Living in the Gift of the Present
Downers Grove, IL: InterVarsity Press, 2013 hb 192 pages $15.00
ISBN 978-0830843077

Juggling life as an English professor, writer, mother, and wife, Weber invites the reader to travel with her as she examines her relationship with Christ in the context of her current life journey. From courageous career choices, to quiet walks in solitude after dinner, to sandy sandwiches on the beach with her children, Weber thoughtfully captures taking leaps of faith as she demonstrates her deepening trust and maturity in Jesus Christ.

The author's message speaks to the conscientious professor, fatigued parent, or writer who is pressed for time. In the interest of full disclosure, I had a personal yearning to read Weber's story of honest struggle after she spent her sabbatical time writing the book at the institution where I currently work. Although female readers, like me, will instantly relate to Weber's journey, her expression of humility, strength, and efforts to find Christ in the ordinary will be attractive to male and female readers alike. In eleven chapters Weber reminds her audience that the work performed in academia is significant, but the steps in an individual's journey to honor and listen to God faithfully are far greater.

Throughout the text, Weber models risk taking in her professional and personal life. On the verge of tenure, she makes the unpopular professional decision to write about her Christian faith in spite of the risk the topic poses at the non-Christian university where she works. While away, she wrestles with how to identify, name, and explore the intersection of her faith, personal life, and scholarship (p. 85). Weber explores her identity in Christ with honesty and humility, giving the professional, the parent, and the scholar permission to do the same. Weber wisely and thoughtfully cautions the reader that the personal and professional choices she makes, although right for her, are not appropriate for all.

The author offers a new perspective on friendship, specifically identifying the importance of what she calls "U-turn friends," or those who will stop what they are doing to help a friend in need. Such friends remind us of what we need to do and where we need to be as individuals in the framework of God's grace. On a personal level, reading chapter four cements Weber's claim for me that authentic, U-turn friends draw us closer and deeper into God's presence (p. 82). She describes Jesus as the ultimate example of a U-turn friend, emphasizing that we are never alone. She also concludes that if we love authentically as U-turn friends, we will multiply God's gift of grace to those around us.

Weber writes elegantly about fellowship, faith, and rest. She writes about finding elements of surprise and gratitude in life's simple pleasures. She finds significant refreshment and renewal in the Lord in simple after-dinner walks. She also skillfully describes her efforts to seize all aspects of each day, recognizing and grasping tightly to the Lord's presence, allowing him to sharpen and refine her rough edges.

Throughout the text Weber affectionately quotes Scripture and her favorite English authors such as Milton, Eliot, Blake, and Lewis, reminding her audience to make connections and look for God and his holiness everywhere. At the end of the text, Weber determines that her sabbatical at a Christian college enriches her connection to the Holy Spirit. While away, she finds gentle renewal in the college's Christian community of fellowship, scholarship, and friendship, all the while discovering a heightened responsibility to live more deliberately, with greater meaning and gratitude, in all aspects of her life, and through all seasons of life (p. 66). One of Weber's greatest lessons includes trusting in Christ's grace with wholehearted obedience as an intentional step to greater spiritual intimacy. I recommend Weber's carefully crafted story to the weary educator looking for a thoughtful yet challenging read that will inspire personal and professional renewal in Christ.

Michelle Hughes

JECB 18:1 (2014): 128–30   1366-5456

Frank Willems
**Stimulating Civic Virtue in Students: An Exploratory Study
of Teachers in Dutch Catholic Primary Education**
Münster: Waxmann, 2013 pb 152pp €25.90
ISBN 978-3-8309-2898-0

A dissertation on citizenship education does not exactly sound stimulating. However, *Stimulating Civic Virtue in Students,* based on a study done in 2009–2010 throughout twenty Dutch Catholic primary schools, serves to promote a virtue-ethical approach to citizenship education in both religious and public school settings. Willems provides a look at teachers' modeling behavior, the moral classroom conversations in which teachers engage, and teachers' moral beliefs about citizenship. This monograph is volume 6 of six in a series entitled Research on Religious and Spiritual Education from the European Association for Research on Learning and Instruction.

The framework for Willems's study is based upon a virtue-ethical approach because "citizenship education is closely linked to moral education" (p. 21). Using this framework, the research conducted was focused on the role of teacher qualities in stimulating civic virtue, the extent to which teachers in Dutch Catholic primary schools embrace their role in teaching virtue, and what can be done to strengthen such teaching in teacher training programs or professional development. While school administration will have an impact on the culture of virtue established in a school, teachers will have the greatest role in developing civic virtue in their students throughout the school day. Teachers have the most direct interaction with primary students, and it follows that they would have the greatest opportunity to have significant impact on the development of virtues in their students.

Willems focused the study on three virtues—justice, tolerance, and solidarity—that align with what he refers to as *Catholic social thinking* and therefore should be present in any Dutch Catholic primary school. Teachers can create significant opportunities for citizenship education for their students. Primarily, these opportunities are centered on creating a moral community, setting a moral example, and then taking time in class to discuss and evaluate morality in light of events and issues. Chapters 3, 4, and 5 each provide the basic research format of introducing a research question, providing a page or two of background, explaining the methods, presenting the data, and discussing the findings. Each of these chapters presents a final section that summarizes "suggestions for educational practice." For me as an educator, the value in reading this book comes from these summaries and the suggestions given for those involved as part of a teacher preparation program.

According to Willems, the key findings that should inform how teachers view their role in civic virtue education are as follows. Students generally see their teachers as more virtuous than the teachers view themselves. However, teacher perception and student perception regarding what is virtuous are not always congruous. As a result, as teachers are reminded that they must model the behavior they expect of their students, they must also be "preaching what they practise" (p. 47). Teachers must also be aware that moral classroom conversations are formative for their students and must plan, prepare, and practice to create discussions that are "more structured, rich and attractive" (p. 61). In an effort to avoid indoctrinating students, teachers often avoid moral conversations. Teachers must be better equipped in their preparation to enter into these conversations in their classroom.

While the study is based on religious schools, Willems offers an extension of the conclusions to public schools in chapter 7. Schooling has a significant impact on primary-age students, and if citizenship education is a stated goal in either a sacred or secular educational setting, teachers must be intentionally prepared to accomplish this goal. Historically, there has been an appeal for civic education in public schools as well as religious schools. Willems believes in, and makes a case for, the general pedagogy and content of the virtue-ethical approach being applicable across faiths and communities.

It is an interesting academic read for those interested in ethics education, especially if one is studying the influence of teachers on their students with regard to citizenship. It is not a stretch in today's educational setting to agree with Willems's belief that school might be "the best place for students to learn what good citizenship means" (p. 9). Given that the text is just over 100 pages long and written in a concise yet informative manner, it is a quick read. For those looking for ideas of how to incorporate citizenship education in teacher preparation programs, it is easy to skim and quickly find the summaries and suggestions of how best to inform and prepare new teachers for modeling and teaching virtue-ethics in a primary classroom. There are some issues in this book similar to those in the more technical title by DeVitas and Yu reviewed in this journal regarding the strengths and weaknesses in character education in American public schools.

Aaron Imig

JECB 18:1 (2014): 130–32   1366-5456

Quentin Wodon
Education in Sub-Saharan Africa: Comparing Faith-Inspired, Private Secular, and Public Schools
Washington, DC: World Bank, 2014 pb 139pp $13.00
ISBN 978-0-8213-9965-1

This remarkably comprehensive study by the World Bank compared government schools, faith-inspired private schools (both Christian and Muslim), and secular private schools across sixteen countries in sub-Saharan Africa. From extensive questionnaires circulated in those countries, the study draws seven findings. Each of these findings is developed in remarkable detail in later chapters, but simply reading them gives one a sense of why this book is interesting. To be sure, schools in sub-Saharan Africa face different challenges and operate in far different contexts than the schools that most of us are familiar with. But the findings are alternately affirming, obvious, perplexing, and challenging. Here are the overall conclusions that the study reached:

1. "Faith-inspired schools enroll 14 percent of all primary students and 11 percent of secondary school students" (p. 1).
2. "The order of magnitude of the market share of private schools is similar to surveys and administrative data, but it is slightly higher in surveys, possibly in part because some private schools operate without official recognition" (p. 3).
3. "Faith-inspired schools tend to reach the poor slightly less than public schools, but much more than private secular schools" (p. 4).
4. "There are large differences in the private costs of education for households between providers, with faith-inspired schools costing more than public schools, but less than private secular schools" (p. 5).
5. "Private secular and faith-inspired schools have substantially higher satisfaction rates among parents than public schools" (p. 7).
6. "Faith and values are key reasons why some parents choose faith-inspired schools with quality also playing a role, especially for the choice of Christian schools" (p. 8).
7. "There is some evidence that students in faith-inspired schools and especially those in private secular schools, perform better than students in public schools, but more research is needed in this area" (p. 10).

As the book delves into each of these findings, the statistical data allow the reader to explore questions and hypotheses they might have about why the results are the way they are. Typically when I read a study, these sorts of questions just hang there. In the case of this study, many of my hypotheses were actually addressed with further statistics on the next page. The discussion in each chapter is comprehensible to those who are not statistics experts. At the same time, other questions are larger and sometimes philosophical. For example, the book suggests that one priority is to "deal with the risk of duplication of efforts and the lack of harmonization between education providers" (p. 11). I found myself wondering what harmonization might mean, and whether diverse populations might not better be served by diverse (and perhaps not fully harmonized) schools.

Wodon also suggests that it should be a priority to understand "the constraints within which private schools and especially the faith-inspired schools that serve the poor operate" (p. 11). I found myself wishing there were such a study looking at the same question for Christian schools in the US, where I teach.

Subsequent chapters delve into data and methodology, market share, reaching the poor and vulnerable, the private cost of education, and parent and student satisfaction and preferences, followed by an excellent conclusion/summary and a series of detailed appendixes. I am used to reading quantitative studies and find I often skip over many sections. This book was written in such a way that the statistical details both illuminate questions and answers, and at the same time, bring up layers of new questions.

Although this is not the sort of book that I usually find myself recommending to a colleague, I found it to be that rarest of rare books, a remarkable detailed quantitative study that somehow functions almost more like a thought-provoking essay, allowing the reader to take a very close look at a Christian school system that he or she is not familiar with, and in so doing, to be able to see the Christian school systems in the reader's homeland from a new, different, and remarkably illuminating perspective.

William Boerman-Cornell

The Journal of Education and Christian Belief

Concerned with current educational thinking from a Christian perspective

ISSN: 1366-5456
http://www.calvin.edu/kuyers/jecb/

SPONSORING BODIES

Association of Christian Teachers
23 Billing Road, Northampton NN1 5AT, United Kingdom
http://www.christian-teachers.org.uk
Kuyers Institute for Christian Teaching and Learning, Calvin College
3201 Burton Street SE, Grand Rapids, MI 49546, USA
http://www.pedagogy.net

INDEXING

This journal is indexed in the British Education Index, Religion Index One: Periodicals (RIO), Religious & Theological Abstracts, Research into Higher Education Abstracts, Educational Research Abstracts Online, a number of EBSCO databases, the Education Resources Information Center (ERIC), and other abstracting and indexing sources.

CURRENT SUBSCRIPTION RATES

	One Year	Two Years	Three Years
Institutions	US $50.00	US $90.00	US $120.00
Individuals	US $39.00	US $69.00	US $99.00

Credit card orders are welcome; if necessary, currency conversion will be performed by the bank issuing the card. Place orders through the Calvin College campus store (Grand Rapids, Michigan, USA), at either http://bit.ly/jecbsubscribe or http://store.calvin.edu.
Full-text online access is available exclusively through EBSCO*host*.

Volume 18, no. 1 (2014)
Copyright © 2014 The Association of Christian Teachers and the Kuyers Institute for Christian Teaching and Learning
ISBN 978-1-937555-53-5   ISSN 1366-5456

EDITORIAL POLICY

The views expressed by individual contributors and books reviewed or advertised in the journal are not necessarily endorsed by the editors, publishers, or sponsoring bodies.

EDITORIAL ADDRESSES

USA and Canada
Dr. David Smith, *JECB* Editor
Kuyers Institute for Christian Teaching and Learning, Calvin College
3201 Burton Street SE, Grand Rapids, MI 49546, USA
E-mail: jecb@calvin.edu

Dr. Ken Badley, *JECB* Reviews Editor
George Fox University School of Education
414 North Meridian Street, Newberg, OR 97132, USA
E-mail: jecb-reviews@calvin.edu

Rest of World
Professor Trevor Cooling, *JECB* Editor
National Institute for Christian Education Research
Canterbury Christ Church University
North Holmes Road, Canterbury, Kent CT1 1QU, United Kingdom
E-mail: jecb-uk@calvin.edu

ARTICLES
Manuscripts of 4,000 to 5,000 words should be submitted as a file in a standard word-processing format to the appropriate editorial e-mail address. Everything, including notes, should be double-spaced. To facilitate anonymous review by referees, the author's name should not appear in the article; please include a separate cover sheet that contains the article title, an abstract of up to 100 words, the author's name and full contact details, a single-sentence institutional affiliation, up to six keywords and phrases that describe the article's focus, and a statement that the article is original and has not been published elsewhere. Contributors should retain copies of their files since the editors can take no responsibility in case of loss or damage. Acceptance of manuscripts is subject to the journal's peer review policy (see http://www.calvin.edu/kuyers/jecb/). Authors should bear in

mind that they are addressing an international readership and either avoid or explain local jargon.

References. Citations should conform to the *Publication Manual of the American Psychological Association* (6th ed., 2nd printing or later). A full bibliography of works cited should appear at the end of the article. Endnotes should be numbered consecutively in the text. If specialized software is used to prepare the citations and bibliography, please convert all fields to editable text before submitting.

BOOK REVIEWS

Books for review should be sent to either Dr. Ken Badley (USA and Canada) or Professor Trevor Cooling (rest of world) at the addresses above. Full instructions to reviewers will be sent together with books for review. Suggestions are welcome from readers regarding books they consider should be reviewed in the journal.

NEWS & NOTES

Items for our News & Notes section should be sent to the editors. Details of publications and major conferences of interest to our readers are particularly welcome.

COPYRIGHT

CPSIA information can be obtained at www.ICGtesting.com
Printed in the USA
BVOW11s2250090614

355883BV00007B/124/P

9 781937 555535